IMAGES
of America

SAN FRANCISCO'S
TWIN PEAKS

In this 1950s aerial map, Twin Peaks (the figure eight formed by Twin Peaks Boulevard encircling the peaks) is surrounded by Clarendon Heights to the north (top) and the Summit and Twin Peaks Reservoirs with Villa, Graystone, and Crown Terraces to the east. Corbett Avenue (known as Corbett Road before 1914) and Upper Market Street wind around the east slope of Twin Peaks, and Midtown Terrace is to the south and west. (Courtesy private collection.)

ON THE COVER: Children take in the downtown city views from the east slope of Twin Peaks in 1928. Situated just below them is a dairy farm surrounded by trees. Acreage from that farm would become Rooftop Elementary School 25 years later. (Courtesy private collection.)

IMAGES
of America

SAN FRANCISCO'S
TWIN PEAKS

Lynn Oakley

ARCADIA
PUBLISHING

Published by Arcadia Publishing
Charleston, South Carolina

Library of Congress Control Number: 2012953501

For all general information, please contact Arcadia Publishing:
Telephone 843-853-2070
Fax 843-853-0044
E-mail sales@arcadiapublishing.com
For customer service and orders:
Toll-Free 1-888-313-2665

Visit us on the Internet at www.arcadiapublishing.com

This book is dedicated to the Twin Peaks Improvement Association and those individuals who have worked in earnest to preserve, protect, and maintain the natural beauty of Twin Peaks.

CONTENTS

ACKNOWLEDGMENTS

It takes the support and input of several people and organizations to launch a book, and I am grateful for all the help I have received. The research into the history of Twin Peaks included many hours of consultation with experts in the fascinating fields of geology, engineering, architecture and urban design, and San Francisco history. Plus, meeting and talking to neighbors added much valuable insight. I would like to thank the following people for their tremendous help with this endeavor: seismic geologist Lloyd Cluff and geologist Gordon Thrupp for their scientific information about the geological history of Twin Peaks; Richard H. Dorman Sr., geologist, project manager, Atlanta Mine, Pioche, Nevada, for sharing his knowledge about engineering and pipes; the knowledgeable staffs at the Bancroft Library and the Environmental Design Archives, University of California, Berkeley; all of the helpful folks at the San Francisco History Center, San Francisco Public Library; Edith Fried for contributing so much to the beauty of the Twin Peaks area in addition to providing some valuable photographs and information for this book; Marian Bernstein, Janet Cluff, Nancy Hogan, Ruth and Oleg Obuhoff, Soc Oulson, Pat Taber, and Rita A. da Luz; Jacqueline Proctor, a fellow Arcadia historian who has also written *Bay Area Beauty, The Artistry of Harold G. Stoner, Architect,* for her encouragement; all of the historians and journalists before me who have left a trail of informative articles about Twin Peaks; Greg Gaar, a naturalist with a great knowledge of San Francisco history and a matching collection of photographs; editor Jared Nelson of Arcadia Publishing for leading me through the process; editor/writer John Skinas for his great knack for grammar and style; and my grandparents Edward and Alice Moffitt and Erwin and Beulah Mehlinger, who settled in the Twin Peaks area and saved valuable photographs and shared their stories of Twin Peaks.

I would especially like to thank my husband, Roy, for his great enthusiasm, suggestions, and support for this project.

INTRODUCTION

Doubly happy . . . is the man to whom lofty mountain tops are within reach.

—John Muir, from *Steep Trails*
Chapter 20: An Ascent of Mount Rainier

Historically, Twin Peaks has been both an iconic landmark for San Franciscans and visitors as well as a challenge to city planners and travelers puzzling over how to circumnavigate these two centrally located hills. Roads and a tunnel were eventually carved into the peaks, facilitating the westward expansion of the city, which connected the bustling eastern section to the underdeveloped western area.

Parades of hikers and bikers and busloads of tourists make their way up to Twin Peaks every day to take in the incredible views. The magnificent 360-degree panorama encompasses the Pacific Ocean to the west, the Golden Gate to the north (a view punctuated by Mount Tamalpais), Mount Diablo to the east, and Mount Hamilton and San Bruno Mountain to the south. From the summit, the city of San Francisco spreads out concentrically below one's feet—a virtual living map of the city.

The height and strong bedrock of Twin Peaks make this area an ideal location for the three water reservoirs located on and near the peaks, providing a gravity-powered water system for fire hydrants below and drinking water for residents. During the 1906 earthquake, the downtown water mains ruptured, making it difficult to fight the resulting fire. This prompted the City of San Francisco to devise a unique gravity-based water system.

Television and radio transmissions originally emanated from the American Broadcasting Company tower that was built next to Adolph Gilbert Sutro's (Adolph Sutro's grandson) mansion in 1948. Sutro Tower, which replaced the ABC tower, has been transmitting for the past 40 years. Both towers were erected on Clarendon Heights Hill (also known as Sutro Crest, which stands at 825 feet) between Twin Peaks and Mount Sutro. The towers on Christmas Tree Point—the primary lookout point—aid police and fire department transmissions.

Hikers and tourists may come to Twin Peaks for the spectacular views, but most of them are probably unaware that they are surrounded by very old, geologically significant marvels. The hills forming Twin Peaks were actually under water 65 to 175 million years ago, as evidenced by the radiolarian ribbon chert and pillow basalt found on them today. Chert, pillow basalt, and serpentine are the "fault-slivered mass of displaced sea rock," according to Keith Heyer Meldahl's book *Rough-Hewn Land: A Geologic Journey from California to the Rocky Mountains*, that make up the Franciscan Complex, a geological marvel known by geologists around the world. At one time, the top of Twin Peaks was located several thousand miles west of San Francisco, deep in the ocean.

The peaks are not identical. The northern peak has bands of red chert, about one to two inches thick, while the southern peak has black to yellow-brown chunks of pillow basalt. The grasses and shrubs associated with chert are found on Twin Peaks, as is the Mission Blue butterfly (*Ocaricia icarioides missionensis*), a federally protected endangered species living in this area of San Francisco as well as parts of Marin County and San Mateo County.

The Ohlone (an Indian word meaning "abalone") people were the earliest Native Americans, also called Costanoans ("coast people") by the Spanish, to inhabit the California coast from San Francisco Bay to the Salinas Valley. Archaeologists estimate that the Ohlones settled in the San Francisco area around AD 500. These natives were hunters, fishermen, and gatherers who most likely foraged on Twin Peaks. According to Ohlone lore, they believed that Twin Peaks was once one mountain peak—a united husband and wife. But because they quarreled too much, the Great Spirit split them with a bolt of lightning, producing a more peaceful environment.

Europeans arrived in the mid-18th century, disrupting the peaceful existence of the Ohlone people. The number of Ohlones living in the area before the Spanish arrived has not been determined precisely but has been estimated as high as 18,200. It is known that huge numbers of them died within the next 40 years from the ravages of European diseases and mistreatment. The Spanish landed in San Francisco Bay in 1769 after sailing up the coast from Monterey on orders from Gen. Juan Bautista de Anza. Under the leadership of Fr. Junipero Serra and Gov. Gaspar de Portola, they began converting natives to Christianity and worked on civilizing the natives. Missions were built up and down the state of California, then known as Alta California. The Mission San Francisco de Asis, or Mission Dolores, and the Presidio de San Francisco were established in 1776. The mission was located near Arroyo de los Dolores, a creek that was fed by the watershed on the eastern slope of Twin Peaks.

Mexico won its independence from Spain in 1821, and California became Mexican territory. The missions were taken over by the Mexican government, which granted large areas of land, called ranchos, to Mexican citizens. In 1845, Gov. Pio Pico awarded Rancho San Miguel to Don Jose de Jesus Noe, who later became the last alcalde (mayor) of Yerba Buena (San Francisco). This was a large land grant of 4,443 acres, which included Twin Peaks, Mount Davidson, Noe Valley, the Castro, Glen Park, Diamond Heights, St. Francis Wood, and Eureka Valley. Noe began selling parts of Rancho San Miguel in 1852, perhaps because of the discovery of gold at Sutter's Mill in addition to his wife's death, leaving him with three sons. In 1857, as a condition of the Mexican-American War by the Land Act of 1851, the United States of America finally ceded this land to him. But by that time he had sold off most of Rancho San Miguel. François Pioche bought a great deal of Rancho San Miguel in 1862; however, he lost it in a foreclosure sale in 1878.

Mayor Adolph Sutro bought the northwestern parcel of the original Rancho San Miguel in 1880. His large ranch extended from University of California, San Francisco (UCSF) on Parnassus Avenue, south along Stanyan Street, over Twin Peaks, south in the Ocean View district, east to Junipero Serra Boulevard, and to Laguna Honda Reservoir. The San Miguel Range—Mount Sutro, Twin Peaks, and Mount Davidson—were part of this parcel, as was Sutro Forest, the trees of which were planted during Adolph Sutro's Arbor Day campaign in 1886.

The son of one of the foremost commanders for the Mexicans, Gen. Mariano Guadalupe Vallejo, who was also instrumental in making California a state in the Union, wrote of Twin Peaks, "Never have I seen a cultured woman half so fair as this untaught, unadorned daughter of the wilds." There were no trees on the peaks at that time, thus it was "unadorned."

The Twin Peaks neighborhood described in this book encompasses two of the highest hills in San Francisco. The two peaks are 922 feet high and located at the heart of San Francisco. Mount Davidson is the highest hill in San Francisco at 928 feet. The scope of this book will focus on the roads and tunnel on Twin Peaks and their resulting farms and neighborhoods: Corbett Heights, Clarendon Heights, Midtown Terrace, and the Villa, Graystone, and Crown Terraces. It will end with a chapter dedicated to the imaginative and beautiful plans by past architects and artists who were inspired to create designs for the summit and slopes of Twin Peaks.

Chert is a sedimentary rock made up of single-celled organisms called radiolaria, which lived in the top 100 meters of the mid-ocean. The shells of these organisms were deposited on the ocean floor. Many layers of this material were deposited on top of each other and pressed together, combined with dust from the earth's surface blown by the tradewinds. Chert, seen in the photograph on the left, is found on the north (Eureka) peak. Pillow basalt originated in the mid-ocean ridge in the igneous deep part of the ocean that ended up on the continental crust and was covered by chert. Underwater volcanic eruptions pushed the ocean plate toward the continent. The cold-water eruptions froze the lava into a bubble or pillow shape. The image on the right is the pillow basalt found on the south (Noe) peak. (Both, author's collection.)

This is an 1816 lithograph by Russian artist Louis Choris from his book *Voyage Pittoresque*, published in 1822. It shows Ohlones on the San Francisco Bay using oars with spears at one end. The Ohlone Indians gathered plants from Twin Peaks for ceremonial and medicinal uses. Their arrowheads were made of chert, which might have come from Twin Peaks. (Courtesy the Bancroft Library, University of California, Berkeley.)

This is a 1880s view of Twin Peaks from Mission Dolores, which was built by the Spanish in 1776. The maps from this period refer to Twin Peaks as Los Pechos de las Choca ("the Breasts of the Indian Woman"). Bayard Taylor wrote in 1849, "Three miles from San Francisco is the old Mission of Dolores situated in a sheltered valley which is watered by a perpetual stream fed from the tall peaks towards the sea." (Courtesy private collection.)

Noe raised cattle and grew wheat and fruit trees on this land. Due to the lack of roads on Twin Peaks, the lands remained farmland and grazing pastures for cattle into the 1930s. This 1880s photograph shows cattle grazing on Twin Peaks before the roads around the peaks were built. (Courtesy private collection.)

One

THE VIEWS

Exploring and foraging on Twin Peaks, the Ohlone Indians would have been able to easily spot game, approaching natives, and changes in the weather. The views spread from Twin Peaks west to the Pacific Ocean, north and east to the bay, and south to the peninsula.

The population of San Francisco has grown considerably from the early Spanish, Mexican, and American colonization in the 1840s. The growth of San Francisco's population has spread concentrically around Twin Peaks, dramatically changing the silhouette of the populated area of the city. San Francisco's population in 2012 was 815,000, making it the second most densely populated city in the United States, second only to New York City. The density was 17,463.22 people per square mile.

Over the past 200 years, artists, cartographers, and photographers have created many images of Twin Peaks as well as the city as seen from Twin Peaks. The Spanish charted the San Francisco Bay in 1775. Louis Choris, a German Russian painter and explorer who accompanied the Romanzoff Expedition to North America and the Pacific Coast in 1816, produced lithographs of the Presidio and the Ohlone Indians. Many early images of a developing San Francisco and Twin Peaks are available thanks to the invention of the camera in the 19th century. Urban designer Daniel Burnham took several photographs of and from Twin Peaks before the earthquake as he formulated a master design for San Francisco and Twin Peaks. Photographer George Lawrence even took aerial images of San Francisco after the 1906 earthquake with the use of kites.

Using historical maps as a reference, these photographs and paintings of and from Twin Peaks provide a dramatic rendering of the history and populating of San Francisco. The peaks remain a constant familiar landmark around which the city has spread.

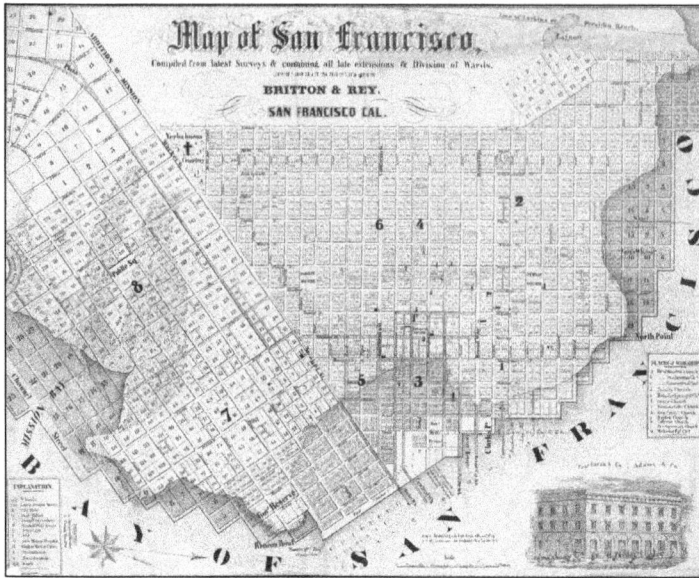

By 1852, the population had grown to 36,151 from 25,000 during the 1849 Gold Rush. San Francisco published its first directory in 1852, listing names and addresses. This 1852 Britton and Rey map of San Francisco shows buildings in the darker areas and indicates the original shoreline. The structure in the lower right of the image was a branch of a St. Louis bank that was ruined in the financial panic of 1855. (Courtesy David Rumsey Map Collection.).

The Bosqui England Printing Company produced this print of San Francisco in 1847, signed by George Hyde, J.D. Stevenson, and Gen. Mariano Vallejo. Twin Peaks can be seen at the upper left, No. 33. The sloop in the middle is the USS *Portsmouth*, the ship that was instrumental in claiming San Francisco for the United States under the command of Capt. John B. Montgomery. (Author's collection.)

By 1870, the population of San Francisco had increased to 149,473, and San Francisco was the 10th largest city in the United States. In 1869, Andrew Smith Hallidie devised a cable car system using wire ropes and a gripping system, which was first installed at the intersection of Clay and Kearny Streets, running to the crest of the hill. This 1872 map is Bancroft's Official Guide Map of the City and County of San Francisco. (Courtesy David Rumsey Map Collection.)

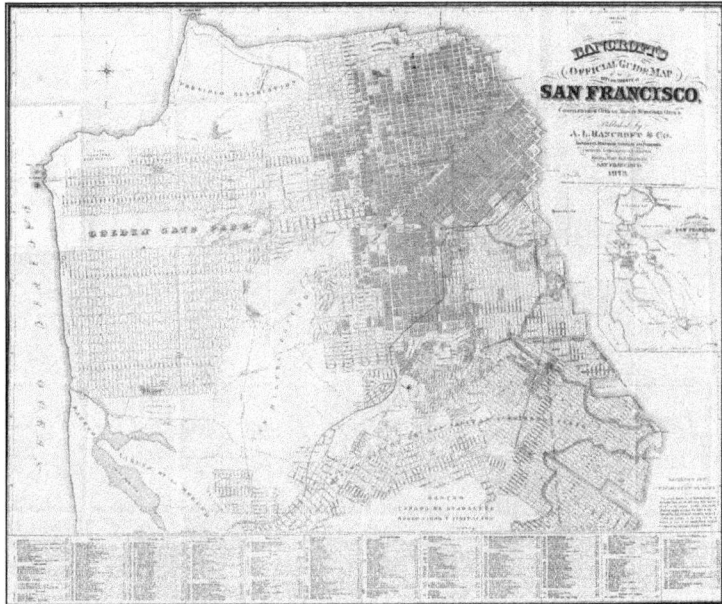

This 1868 aerial map by George H. Goddard shows the Golden Gate and the bay with San Francisco in the foreground. Market Street is represented by the diagonal line, leading from the Ferry Building down toward the right to Twin Peaks. (Courtesy David Rumsey Map Collection.)

This 1872 view of San Francisco from Twin Peaks looks east past farms on the slopes and down unpaved Market Street. Right in the middle of this photograph, blocking Market Street, is an enormous sand pile, one of many that were on or near Market Street. There was also a 60-foot-tall sand hill near where the Palace Hotel is located today. The sand was eventually removed by the use of "paddies," steam shovels with movable tracks that hauled the sand away. The sand was used to fill in the marshes along the South of Market area and to level Market Street itself. What was left of Lake McCoppin, a swampy area between Seventeenth and Nineteenth Streets, south of Eighteenth Street, was filled in. (Courtesy private collection.)

This 1880s photograph from Twin Peaks shows a still unpaved Market Street and more homes creeping closer to the peaks. In 1879, Pres. Ulysses S. Grant was honored with a parade down Market Street. Future presidents Hayes, Harrison, McKinley, Roosevelt, and Taft were also accorded this honor. An 1883 grand procession of the Knights Templar dressed in full regalia, complete with horses and decorations, marched down Market Street and was viewed by the whole city plus 70,000 visitors. (Courtesy private collection.)

Twin Peaks is to the right as seen from a hill near Golden Gate Park on October 31, 1886. The dairy farm on the eastern slope of Twin Peaks is where Rooftop Elementary School is located today. Corbett Road can barely be seen leading up to the farm from the right. An advertisement appeared in the 1899 *San Francisco Call* that read, "Ranch Hand; must be a good milker, Twin Peaks Dairy, Corbett Road." (Courtesy private collection.)

This view of Twin Peaks in the late 1800s was most likely taken from Market Street near Castro Street. The trees surrounding the dairy farm have grown quite a bit from the previous 1886 photograph. (Courtesy private collection.)

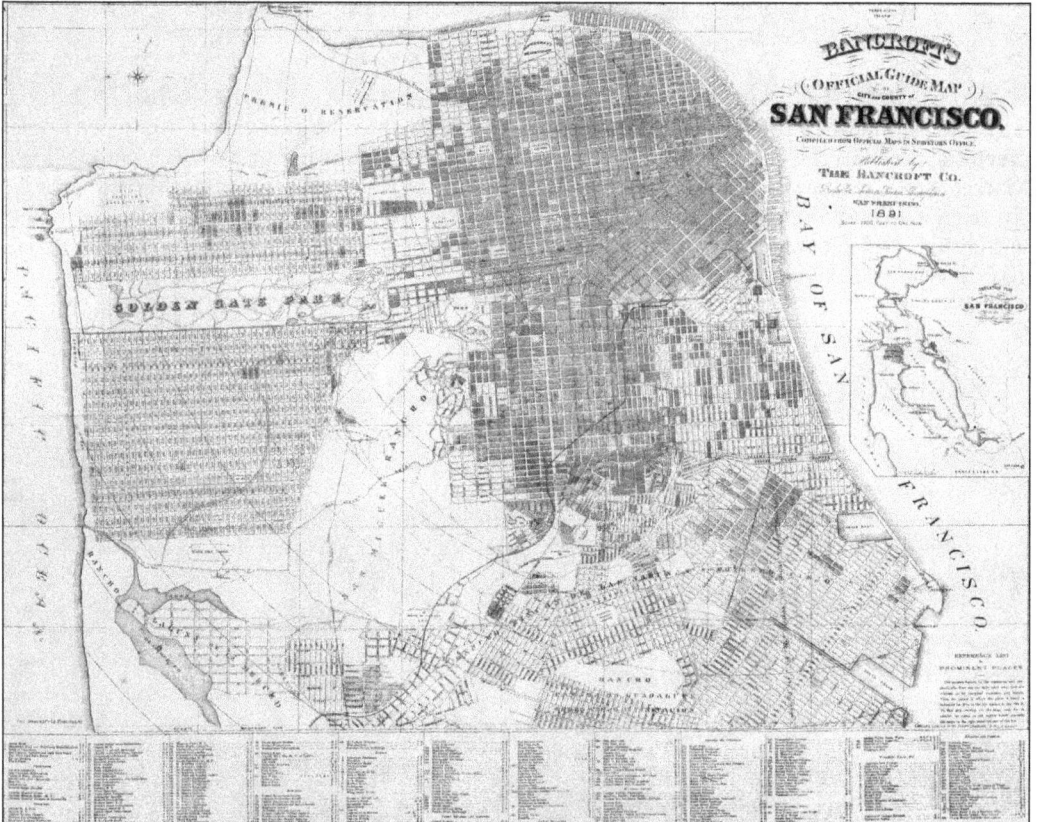

In 1900, the population of San Francisco was 342,782. The bubonic plague from 1900 to 1904 erupted in Chinatown. Pres. William McKinley was assassinated in 1901, and Theodore Roosevelt became president. This 1891 Bancroft map shows new development beginning to push westward around Twin Peaks. The concentric circles indicate the distance from the Ferry Building. The downtown area is filled in solidly with buildings. (Courtesy David Rumsey Map Collection.)

This is a 1905 photograph of Twin Peaks from Twenty-third and Howard Streets. The peaks are still bare, and Twin Peaks Boulevard had not yet been constructed around the peaks. Horse-drawn carriages are still being used on this unpaved road. There are electric wires and gas lamps along the street. (Courtesy David Rumsey Map Collection.)

Daniel Burnham took this 1905 photograph of Twin Peaks from Market Street in preparation for his urban design for San Francisco. Cable cars share the road with horse-drawn carriages. Horse-drawn omnibuses were used until 1905. In 1893, electric streetcars appeared with electric motors powered from lines running above, gradually replacing the cable cars on Market Street. These cable cars appear to be pulled by a cable in the track. (Courtesy David Rumsey Map Collection.)

Following the devastating earthquake of April 18, 1906, several fires started from ruptured gas lines. One was the famous "ham and eggs fire," started by a woman cooking. And fires erupted as a result of the dynamiting used to create firebreaks. The city burned for four days and nights. The fire was difficult to control because of ruptured water mains. Ninety percent of the destruction was from the fire. The combined effect of the earthquake and fire resulted in 490 city blocks damaged,

Market Street leads from the burned area of the city up toward Twin Peaks following the 1906 earthquake and fire. The dairy farm that eventually became Rooftop Elementary School is located on the land surrounded by the grove of trees in the foreground. (Courtesy private collection.)

25,000 buildings destroyed, and 3,000 people killed. Four square miles, or over 80 percent, of the city was affected. Approximately 227,000 people were left homeless out of a population of about 400,000, and after two years, the refugee camps were still being used at full capacity. This is a view of the fire from Twin Peaks. (Public domain photograph.)

The Pickard family camped on Twin Peaks following the earthquake. After the earthquake, approximately 75,000 refugees left the city. Those who chose to remain sought sanctuary in Golden Gate Park, the Presidio, the Ingleside Racetrack, and other parks as well as Twin Peaks because of its abundant water and agriculture. Many decided to stay. (Courtesy San Francisco History Center, San Francisco Public Library.)

Twin Peaks was often used for advertising because it could be seen from all of downtown. In this 1915 photograph, there is an advertisement for a candidate for sheriff. The building in the foreground is the Humboldt Bank Building at 785 Market Street, celebrating the new year of 1915. Plans for this building, designed by architect Frederick Herman Meyer, began in 1905. Despite the devastation of the earthquake, construction continued and was completed in 1908. (Courtesy private collection.)

Looking north from Clarendon Heights in 1915, there is no Golden Gate Bridge and the Presidio acreage is empty of homes. Just below this location are empty lots that are filled today. (Courtesy private collection.)

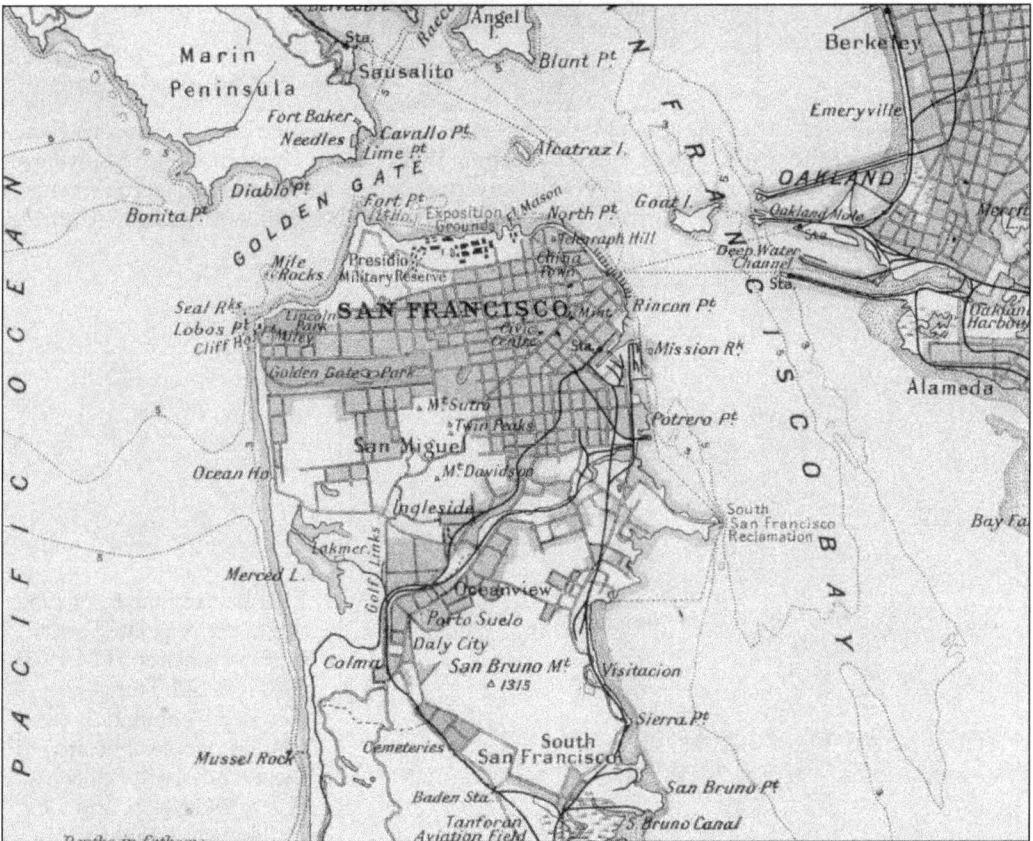

In 1920, the population of San Francisco was 506,676. San Francisco soldiers returned from World War I in 1918 and 1919. "After the war . . . came the peace, and the hunt for a job," wrote Twin Peaks settler Edward Moffitt, the author's grandfather, on his return from France. The men came home to a city that had literally doubled with the construction of Twin Peaks Boulevard and the Twin Peaks Tunnel. This 1922 map by J.G. Bartholomew shows the parts of San Francisco (gray areas) that had been developed. (Courtesy David Rumsey Map Collection.)

This is a 1920s view of Twin Peaks from Market Street. Twin Peaks Boulevard has been constructed around the tops of the peaks, and homes are creeping higher up the eastern slopes. Many farms can be seen along Corbett Road to the left of the pine trees on the eastern slope. Electric streetcars have replaced cable cars on Market Street, but there are still a few horse-drawn carriages. (Courtesy private collection.)

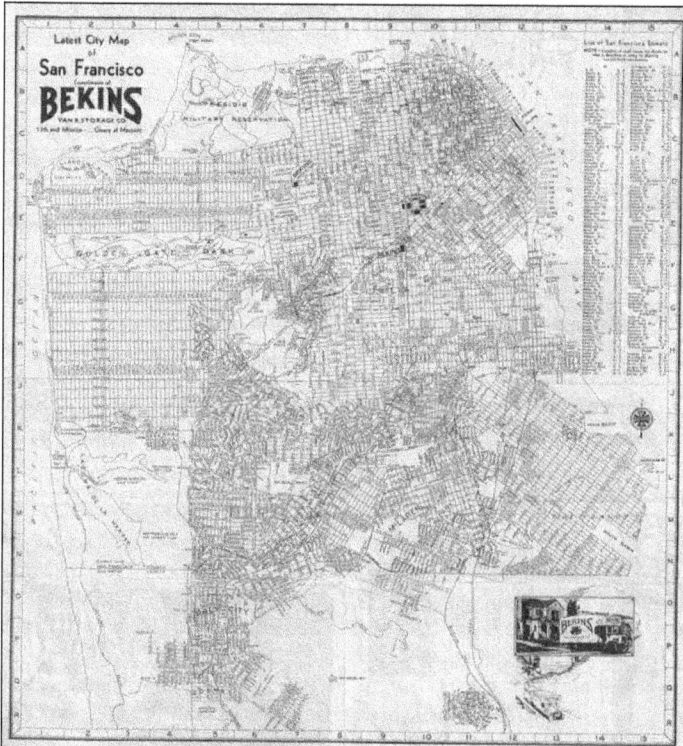

This Bekins map from 1930 shows the populated areas in San Francisco. The 1930 census of San Francisco recorded a population of 634,394 people. The area to the west of Twin Peaks had begun to develop, and City College was established in 1935. The San Francisco Ballet was founded in 1933 as the San Francisco Opera Ballet. Alcatraz became a prison in 1933. (Courtesy Geographicus.)

This 1930 view from Twin Peaks of the downtown area is minus the Bay Bridge. Construction on the bridge began in 1933, and it opened in 1936. The Ferry Building can be seen at the end of Market Street, which has been extended up and around Twin Peaks. (Courtesy private collection.)

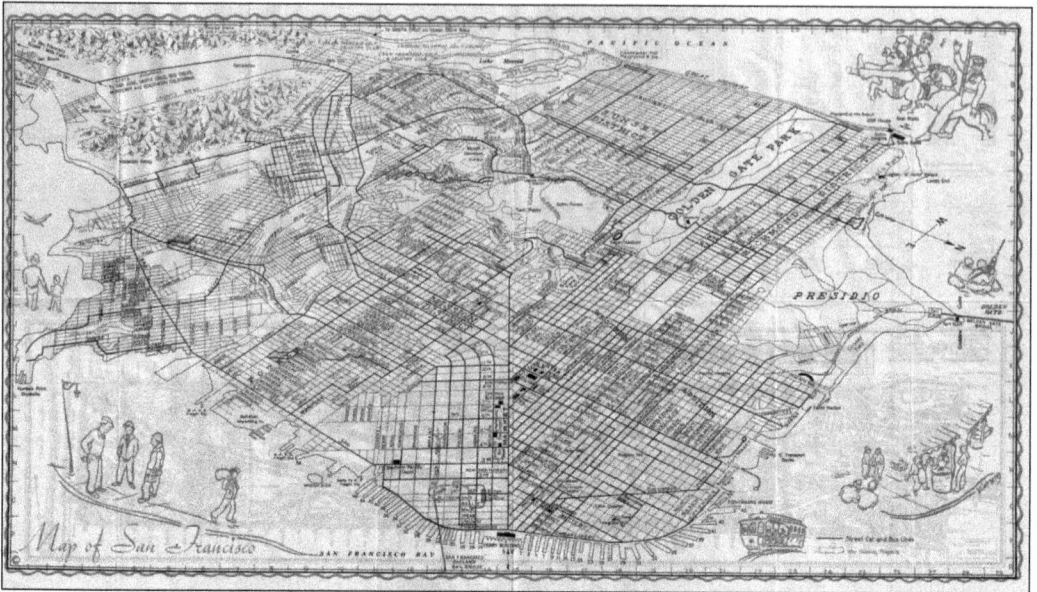

This is a Delkin map of San Francisco in 1940. The population of San Francisco was 634,536. America joined World War II following the Pearl Harbor attack on December 8, 1941. San Francisco relocated Japanese Americans to internment camps in 1942, and the United Nations Charter was signed in San Francisco in 1945. (Courtesy Geographicus.)

San Francisco had a newly built Bay Bridge that opened on November 12, 1936, in time for the Golden Gate International Exposition in 1939 and 1940 on Treasure Island. The buildings from the exposition can be seen in the upper left of this photograph. The Golden Gate International Exposition celebrated the completion of San Francisco's two new, and structurally interesting, bridges. (Courtesy private collection.)

24

This is a 1956 Shell Oil map of San Francisco. The inhabited part of San Francisco has spread around Twin Peaks to the west and south toward the peninsula. Soldiers have come home from World War II, and homes are being built. Midtown Terrace has been developed on the south and west sides of Twin Peaks. (Courtesy David Rumsey Map Collection.)

This 1955 aerial view of Twin Peaks shows the round Twin Peaks Reservoir and just the edges of Summit and Sutro Reservoirs. Midtown Terrace is being developed on the western and southern sides of Twin Peaks, and Twin Peaks Boulevard encircles the peaks. Corbett Avenue runs just below Twin Peaks Boulevard on the eastern slope, and the Market Street extension winds up the hill around Twin Peaks to connect with Portola Drive. (Courtesy San Francisco History Center, San Francisco Public Library.)

Two

There's Water in "Them Thar Hills"

Three reservoirs have been built into the bedrock on Twin Peaks: Twin Peaks, Summit, and Sutro Reservoirs. There were also two tanks: the Clarendon Heights Water Tank (on Tank Hill) and the Ashbury Tank. But natural springs also flow off the peaks, hence the name of one of the streets on Twin Peaks, Mountain Spring Avenue. Water can still be heard constantly running in a culvert at the end of Mountain Spring Avenue. In 1867, Behrend Joost started the Mountain Spring Water Company and sold water from a surface spring at Clayton Street and Corbett Road by the bucket and cup. It was reported at the time that the springwater was sweet and that horses loved it. To this day, streams of water can still be seen flowing down the road at the intersection of Clayton Street and Corbett Avenue as well as on Twin Peaks Boulevard and other hilly roads.

The 1906 earthquake ruptured and twisted the water mains in San Francisco, making it virtually impossible to fight the resulting devastating fire. Determined not to have this happen again, the city made plans for a reservoir to be built on the bedrock on Twin Peaks. It was developed with a $5.2 million bond issue approved by the voters of San Francisco in 1908. Two more reservoirs and a tank were later added to Twin Peaks. Clarendon Heights Tank (on Tank Hill) had already been built in 1894.

This reservoir system uses gravity, which is why Twin Peaks Reservoir is located high on Twin Peaks. The upper zone includes the reservoirs and tank, and the lower zone includes 175 underground cisterns, each holding approximately 75,000 gallons of water. They are found at intersections and indicated by large brick circles in the street with a manhole in the center. There are two pump stations that can assist the process: one at Second and Townsend Streets and one at Van Ness Avenue near Fort Mason. In addition, fireboats can pump saltwater in as needed, thus creating a combination of defenses against the ravages of earthquake and fire.

The Behrend Joost house, located on the Market Street extension, is also known as the Miller-Joost home. Behrend Joost married Anna Miller, whose family owned this home and a dairy farm on Corbett Road. The property for this home, with prize-winning weeping willows, was part of Rancho San Miguel, and Adam Miller bought it from Francois Pioche and Lester Robinson. (Photograph by Alvis Hendley.)

This 1906 view of Alfred "Nobby" Clarke's mansion shows that it was located below Behrend Joost's home between Douglass and Caselli Streets. The spired tower on Clarke's home can be seen in the lower left of the photograph. Springwater flowed from Joost's property down to the land owned by Clarke. They feuded over water rights on Twin Peaks and the distribution of water to Eureka Valley. The escalation of this feud actually ruined both businesses. (Courtesy private collection.)

This early-20th-century view of Clayton Street at Corbett Road, shows the muddied street where the Mountain Spring Water Company was established. At one time, a bridge was constructed so that pedestrians could navigate the intersection without traipsing through the mud. Tracks can be seen where an electric railway ran from Falcon Street to Golden Gate Park in 1886. Falcon Street was later changed to Market Street. The fourth house from the left, which is still standing today, was built in 1908. (Courtesy private collection.)

Streams of water can still be seen today, trickling from the hillside down onto Clayton Street at Corbett Avenue. This is a 2012 view of the same intersection. Corbett Road dairy farms have been replaced with a few homes and many duplexes, fourplexes, and apartment buildings. The small home with slanted roof in the middle of this photograph was built in 1908 and can be seen in the previous image. (Author's collection.)

The intersection at Clayton Street and Corbett Avenue is still occasionally flooded with springwater from the hill, as it was in the days of the Mountain Spring Water Company. This view of the springs flooding the street was taken from Clayton Street and looks down toward Corbett Avenue. Beyond the intersection is the switchback on Market Street. (Courtesy Nancy Hogan collection.)

This 1930s aerial photograph shows the round Twin Peaks Reservoir at lower left and Tank Hill in the upper center. Some repair work was done on the Twin Peaks Reservoir at this time, which is probably why one half appears to be empty. (Courtesy private collection.)

This 1910 photograph shows the Twin Peaks Reservoir construction at the location originally chosen in the 1890s by Fire Chief Dennis T. Sullivan. Construction began in 1909 at an elevation of 758 feet. Michael O'Shaughnessy, the chief engineer for San Francisco in 1912, supervised the building of the Twin Peaks Reservoir as well as the Twin Peaks and Stockton Tunnels, the Municipal Railway System, and the 1915 Panama-Pacific International Exposition. (Courtesy private collection.)

These construction workers stand at the base of the Twin Peaks Reservoir by the entrance to the reservoir tunnel in 1910. The 5,047-square-foot tunnel is used for maintenance and repair of the reservoir. The reservoir is the main part of the Auxiliary Water Supply System (AWSS) that would be capable of covering a city block (100,000 square feet) with 25 feet of water in just one day. (Courtesy private collection.)

The Twin Peaks Reservoir feeds down into the 500,000-gallon tank in Ashbury Heights, which in turn feeds into the 750,000 gallons tank on Jones Street on Nob Hill. The reservoir is constructed with six-inch reinforced concrete slabs. This AWSS remains the only high-pressure network of its type in the United States. (Courtesy private collection.)

The Twin Peaks Reservoir has a 10 million gallon capacity and 150 miles of high-pressure mains with a dam across its center. Each bay is emptied separately. If a pipe breaks, then only half will be lost. The reservoir is supplied with freshwater from the city's water system. Saltwater is destructive to fire-fighting equipment, so it is not used even though it is better at extinguishing fires. (Courtesy private collection.)

This pipe being laid on Corbett Avenue was most likely made of redwood because of its resistance to corrosion and rotting. The inner width of the stave, the wood strips making up the pipe, would be small so that it would fit securely and be more watertight and stronger—similar to how a wood barrel is made. The pipe was then wrapped with steel or iron bands. (Courtesy private collection.)

San Franciscans cross the peaks for the dedication of the new Twin Peaks Reservoir on May 12, 1912. Some carry flags, and many have picnic lunches with them. The opening was delayed by eight days because when one side was filled, it leaked. Using cement, sand, and hydrated lime, the leak was stopped by the Lilley and Thurston Company of San Francisco. (Courtesy private collection.)

The Twin Peaks Reservoir opened on May 12, 1912, with a spectacular ceremony complete with 100 American flags attached around the rim, speeches by politicians, songs and bands, divers, and marathon racers running up from Noe and Eureka Valleys. In the late afternoon, a dance was held inside the empty half of the reservoir. (Courtesy private collection.)

San Franciscans were coming out of a difficult period following the 1906 earthquake and fire and looked forward to having some fun. Plus, they were celebrating the construction of a firefighting system that they hoped would keep them safe. The 1906 fire was the sixth time since 1849 that the city had burned to the ground. Insurance rates had soared, and in some places, insurance was unobtainable. (Courtesy private collection.)

After the dance, the other side of the reservoir was filled with water. The Twin Peaks Reservoir is still a major component of the AWSS. When the 1906 fire happened, 25,000 buildings burned and 80 percent of the entire city's property value was devalued. This reservoir, built in the shape of an ellipse, is 275 by 281 feet and 32 feet deep. (Courtesy private collection.)

The Summit Reservoir, built in 1954 to hold drinking water, sits on Clarendon Heights Hill, nestled between Twin Peaks and Mount Sutro. This reservoir holds 14 million gallons of water. In March 2004, a seismic and water circulation upgrade took place as part of the Water System Improvement Program, and the reservoir was returned to service in August 2006. (Author's collection.)

Midtown Terrace was carved out of the southwest side of Twin Peaks in the early 1950s. The large pit on the right is where the covered Sutro Reservoir was later built. (Courtesy private collection.)

The Sutro Reservoir, built in 1952, is used for drinking water. It holds 32 million gallons of water and is being seismically upgraded with an estimated finishing date of 2014 or 2015. The roof and its supporting structures and foundation will be improved. This is the last reservoir in San Francisco to be updated under the Water System Improvement Program. (Author's collection.)

This photograph shows the 1911 construction of the Ashbury Heights tank on Clayton Street at 495 feet elevation. It is made of riveted steel on a reinforced concrete base and holds 500,000 gallons of water, supplying water to the upper zone (elevations above 150 feet). The riveted steel took four highly skilled riveters to install a rivet into a joint. (Courtesy private collection.)

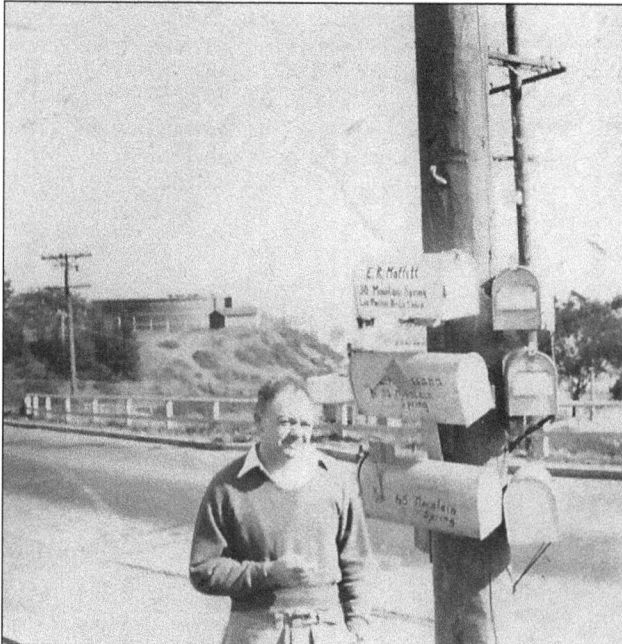

Edward Moffitt, who built the highest house in San Francisco on Twin Peaks in 1922, stands on Twin Peaks Boulevard in 1934 with Tank Hill in the background. The tank was built in 1894 by the Spring Valley Water Company. Drinking water pumped from Laguna Honda was stored in this tank. It became city property in 1930, and the tank was removed in 1957. (Author's collection.)

Members of a neighborhood baseball team have their image captured while sitting on the rocks on top of 650-feet-high Tank Hill, with downtown San Francisco behind them. In 1960, Tank Hill was sold for $230,000 to developers who had plans for building 20 homes on it. But in 1977, it was saved from development by the Open Space Program, through which the city bought Tank Hill for $650,000. (Courtesy private collection.)

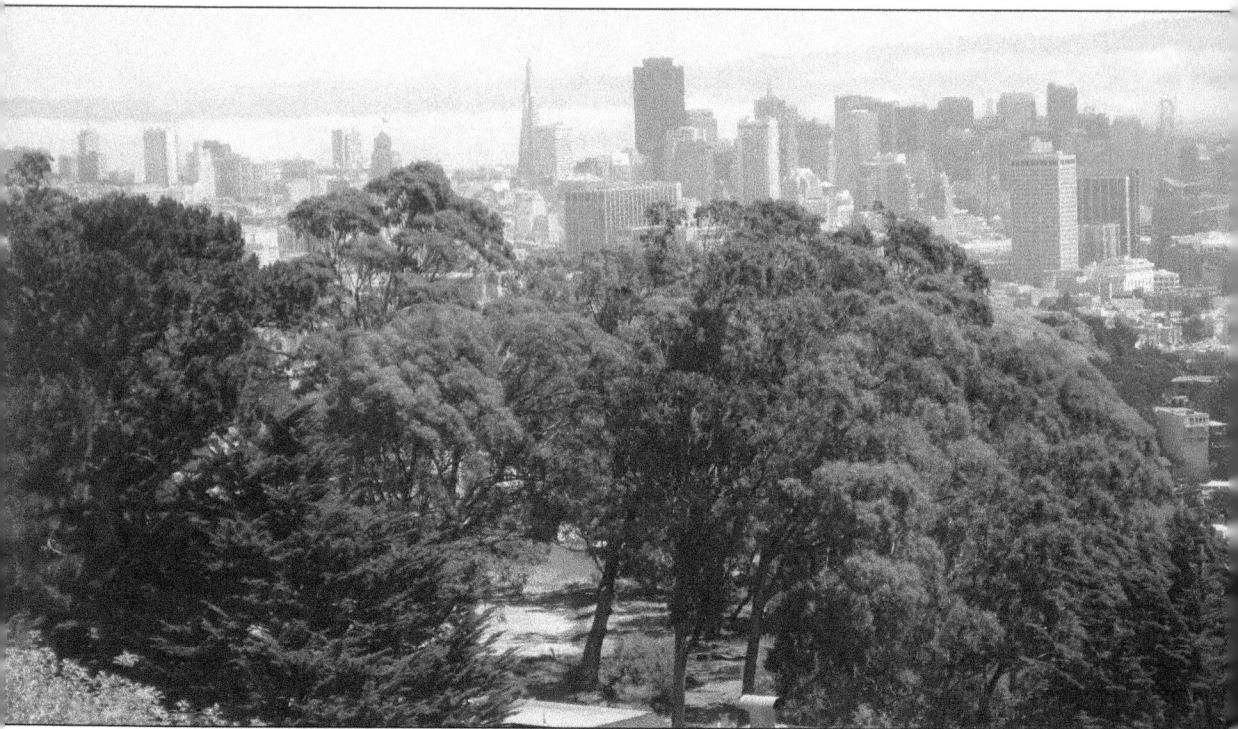

This is a 2012 view of Tank Hill, well adorned with eucalyptus and other varieties of trees. Originally, Tank Hill had very few trees on it, but after the Pearl Harbor attack, eucalyptus trees were reportedly planted to conceal the water tank from Japanese planes. Besides the 60 varieties of native plants, there are garter snakes, alligator lizards, western meadowlarks, kestrels, and hawks that live on the hill. (Author's collection.)

Three

TRAVERSING THE PEAKS

The western part of San Francisco, situated west of Twin Peaks, beckoned to citified San Franciscans with its attractive beaches, wildflower fields, roadhouses, dog and horse racetracks, and shooting ranges in the mid- to late 1800s and early 1900s. The Beach and Ocean Horse Race Course opened in 1865, just south of where Sigmund Stern Grove is located now. Near this racetrack was the Lake House, which was the location for a duel between US senator David Broderick and California Supreme Court justice David Terry in 1859. Customers flocked to the Ocean House, owned by Col. James R. Dickey, and the Beach House, built by Leeson G. Simmons in 1851. Adolph Sutro began building his railroad out to the Cliff House in 1888, accessing the northwest part of town.

The Ingleside Racetrack opened on November 28, 1895, with horse races, which were followed by auto races beginning in 1900. These races were popular and attracted as many as 50,000 spectators. Women wore their finest gowns, decorated with jewels and feathers. From 6:00 a.m. until 1:00 or 2:00 in the afternoon, carriages and horses rode by the various roadhouses on their way to the racetrack, stopping at the intersection of Ocean Avenue and Junipero Serra Boulevard to rest their horses and get a drink at Farley's saloon.

However, there was often a terrific logjam at the end of each race as the carriages attempted to leave at the same time. The wagon wheels interlocked, horses kicked, and many drivers were anxious and frustrated. As early as 1891, surveyor Michael Maurice O'Shaughnessy was hired to make surveys for a possible extension of Market Street over the top of Twin Peaks to the Pacific Ocean in order to ease the way to the west. The addition of Corbett Road, Twin Peaks Boulevard, the Twin Peaks Tunnel, and later the Market Street extension made it possible to get to the west end of San Francisco and literally doubled the populated size of San Francisco. Once those routes were completed, homes and businesses sprang up in the area west of Twin Peaks.

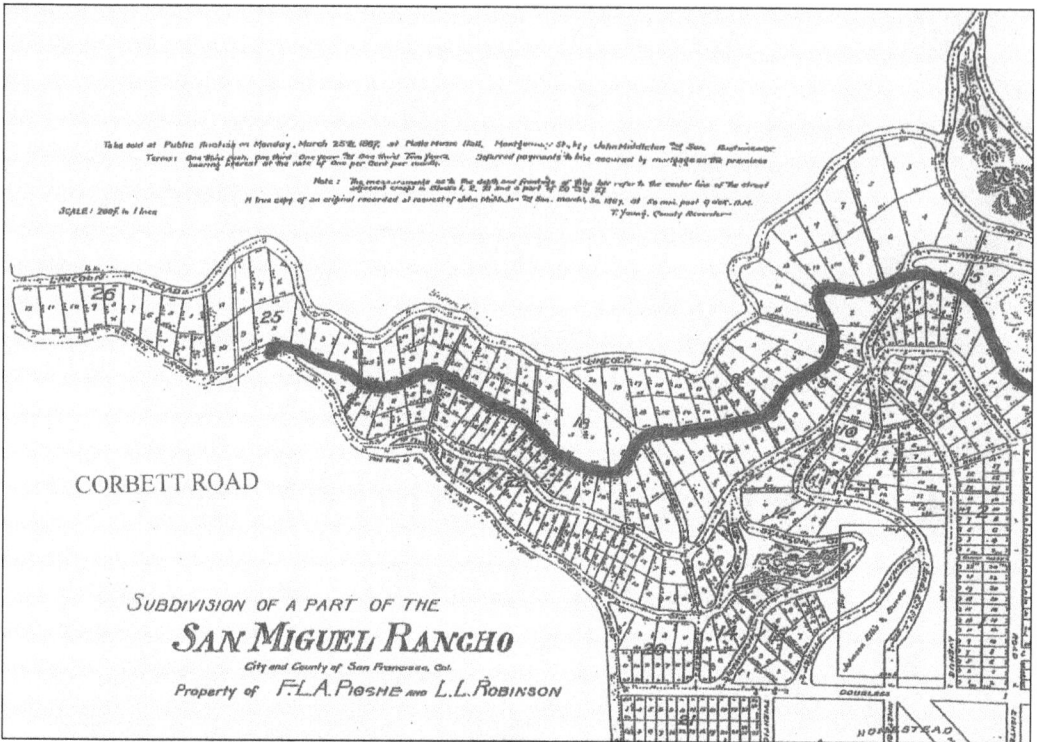

Corbett Avenue has had three designations: road, street, and avenue and three locations. The original Corbett Street was constructed in 1854 and ran from Castro Street to Harrison Street. The name was changed to Corbett Road in 1860, when it became part of a subdivision owned by Francois Pioche and Lester Robinson, as shown on this map. This Corbett Road began at Seventeenth and Douglass Streets, intersected Clayton Street, and ended at Falcon Street. Falcon Street later became Market Street. Corbett Road became Corbett Avenue sometime around 1914, as it appeared in Municipal Reports of that time. (Courtesy Nancy Hogan collection.)

This view of the second Corbett Road area is just past where it intersected Ocean Road, which led out to the beach along what is now known as Portola Drive. (Courtesy private collection.)

Corbett Road was sold in 1862 to attorney William Fitch, who extended this third Corbett Road in 1872 to meet what is now Portola Drive and on to Junipero Serra Boulevard and Ocean Avenue. He formed the Mission and Ocean Beach Macadamized Road Company and turned the road into a toll road, installing a tollgate at Falcon Street, which later became Market Street, and Corbett Road, located on the left side of this photograph. (Courtesy private collection.)

This is a photograph of Camp Ingleside, the 1906 refugee camp at Ingleside racetrack, the destination of many travelers on Corbett Road in the late 19th and early 20th centuries. The Ingleside racetrack was used as a refugee camp and extension of the Laguna Honda following the 1906 earthquake and fire. In 1910, the track was bought and developed by the Urban Realty Development Company, resulting in Ingleside Terraces, a residential community. (Courtesy San Francisco History Center, San Francisco Public Library.)

Farms appeared along Corbett Road in the late 19th century. The toll for the two- to three-mile trip was 10¢ for a saddled horse; 25¢ for a one-horse, one-seat carriage; 25¢ for a two-horse, one-seat carriage; 40¢ for a two-horse, two- or more seat carriage; and 50¢ for a four-horse carriage. This was farm area, so loose cattle, sheep, and hogs were free. (Courtesy private collection.)

The board of supervisors passed a resolution in 1876 to stop the unpopular tolls of 1872 because the road had not been kept up and maintained. Fitch was paid $28,730 in gold coins for his expenses, and the city took ownership of the road in 1877. The road remained free as a public highway. This is Corbett Road in the late 19th century with Diamond Heights in the background. (Courtesy private collection.)

The Twin Peaks Stage Line is picking up passengers on the western side of Tank Hill near where Belgrave Avenue and Stanyan Street are located. The Almshouse Road was a dirt road, just above Cole Valley, that led up the hill to Clarendon Heights, where Clarendon Street is located now. The road then followed Clarendon down to the Almshouse, later known as Laguna Honda Hospital. (Courtesy San Francisco History Center, San Francisco Public Library.)

The Almshouse was nestled into the western base of Twin Peaks, next to where Midtown Terrace is located today. Today, it is called Laguna Honda Hospital. Almshouse Road provided the access from downtown, running between Mount Sutro and Clarendon Heights. Following the devastation of the earthquake and fire in 1906, the Almshouse was used to take care of displaced San Franciscans. (Courtesy private collection.)

This photograph shows dairy farms on Corbett Road near Hopkins Street. For a century, San Francisco produced much of the milk in the California dairy industry, and by 1875, there were nearly 150 milk dealers in San Francisco. In 1888, around 7,000 to 8,000 cows lived within the city limits. By 1904, this number decreased to 4,200. In 1909, the city passed an ordinance allowing no more than two cows per acre. (Courtesy private collection.)

This is the same location at Corbett Avenue, as it is now known, near Hopkins Street in 2012. The farms have long since been replaced by apartment buildings and homes, and the smaller of the trees in the previous photograph have grown quite a bit. (Author's collection.)

These early-1900s travelers are experiencing engine problems on the Corbett Road. There were not many garages in 1902, and it was difficult to get gasoline, which was purchased in drugstores for 60¢ a gallon. Motorists usually carried two five-gallon cans of gas and a gallon of oil in reserve. Automobile contests were held on San Francisco hills for stamina, economy runs, and hill-climbing performances. (Courtesy private collection.)

12778 10-12-30 CORBETT AVE. N. FROM XIE ALLEY

Corbett Avenue was paved on October 12, 1930, near where Rooftop Elementary School is located today at Dixie Alley. The road name was changed to Corbett Avenue as reported in Municipal Reports in 1914. The route reverted to the Pioche and Robinson design beginning at Seventeenth and Douglass Streets and ending at the Market Street extension. When the Market Street extension was planned, it was suggested that Corbett Avenue be widened and straightened as part of this project. Nevertheless, it still has a winding, country feeling. (Courtesy private collection.)

Behrend and Isaac Joost designed, organized, and built San Francisco's first electric railway: the San Francisco & San Mateo (SF&SM) Railway Company. It opened in 1892 and proceeded from Steuart and Market Streets to Daley's Hill, now known as Daly City. The railroad was losing money, so the Joost brothers sold the railway to John Spreckels and his brothers in a foreclosure sale in 1896. (Author's collection.)

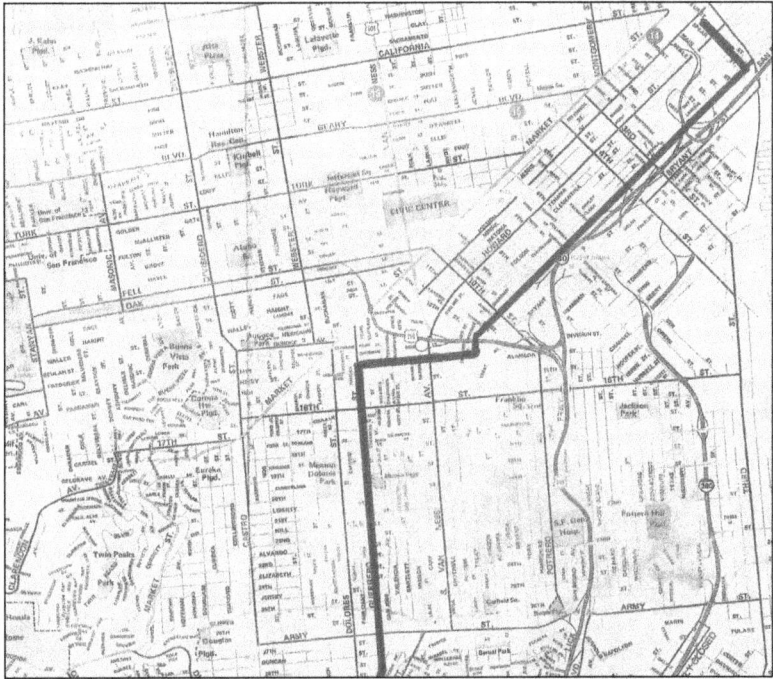

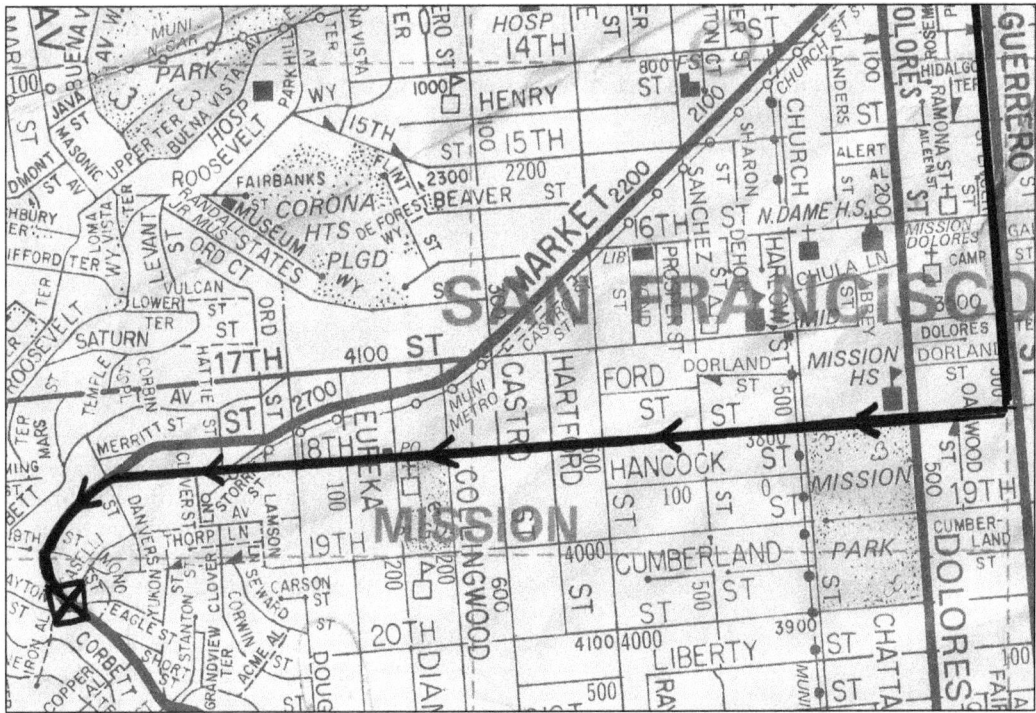

In 1906, after the earthquake, the Spreckels brothers added two lines, one of which started at Guerrero Street, went up Eighteenth Street, and ended at the switchback at Falcon Street, which later became Market Street, and the other line that extended to Golden Gate Park. This map shows the line that extended to the switchback at Falcon Street. (Author's collection.)

The early streetcars that traveled on the slopes of Twin Peaks resembled the cable cars on California Street, as they had two open ends and a center-enclosed section and were called the "California-type car." This photograph shows one of the cars at what is now Market and Clayton Streets, where the switchback was located. (Courtesy private collection.)

The darker line with arrows on the map at the bottom of page 49 shows the route of the switchback. In 1934, the 33 Muni line was famous for its Upper Market Street switchback that enabled the line to climb the lower slopes of Twin Peaks. A curve at Market and Clayton Streets would be too sharp for cars to negotiate. A streetcar is seen in the distance below Tank Hill, running past backyard clotheslines. (Courtesy private collection.)

The benefit of a tunnel was explained in a July 9, 1910, article in the *San Francisco Call*: "By extending Market street through the Twin Peaks this . . . would be only 20 minutes from Third and Kearny streets, thus making it nearer than any suburban town or city. The result will be the building up of one-fourth of the city, which is now in a dormant state because of lack of adequate transportation facilities. Rapid transit is the cause of the growth of all cities."

PROPOSED PLAN FOR TWIN PEAKS TUNNEL AND OBSERVATORY

One plan called for an observatory on top of Twin Peaks in addition to the tunnel through the hills. When it was completed, the Twin Peaks Tunnel was considered one of the longest railway tunnels in the world at 12,000 feet, starting on Market Street and ending at West Portal. At first, streetcars were used, and then light rail was used with an exclusive right-of-way and higher speed. The final contract cost was $3,947,856.70. (Courtesy private collection.)

This is the entrance of the Twin Peaks Tunnel at Castro and Market Streets. The Twin Peaks Tunnel's construction began on November 30, 1914, and was completed July 14, 1917, opening on February 3, 1918. It took 1,000 days to build the tunnel, and three men were fatally injured by a delayed blast during the dynamiting phase. Despite the sacrifices, the Twin Peaks Tunnel was a huge benefit to the city. (Courtesy San Francisco History Center, San Francisco Public Library.)

The exit point of the Twin Peaks Tunnel surfaced at West Portal. Four owners of large real estate tracts west of Twin Peaks helped with the financing of this project: A.S. Baldwin, Joseph Leonard, J.E. Greene, and Duncan McDuffie, who planned St. Francis Wood. The sign to the right of the tunnel entrance reads Claremont Station, First Daylight Stop, 17 minutes to Kearny Street. (Courtesy San Francisco History Center, San Francisco Public Library.)

In 1910, the population of San Francisco was 416,912. The population nearly doubled after the completion of the tunnel, integrating the area west of Twin Peaks with the eastern side. San Francisco mayor James Rolph remarked at the July 14, 1918, dedication of the tunnel, "Westward the course of Empire takes it way" and called the project "bully." (Courtesy San Francisco History Center, San Francisco Public Library.)

In 1916, Fernando Nelson & Sons bought 49 acres next to the western entrance of the Twin Peaks Tunnel for $300,000. It was called West Portal Park and is now known as simply West Portal. Property values increased. Land in the first block near the southwest portal rose from $20 a frontage foot in 1912 to $500 per frontage foot in 1930. This is an August 4, 1945, view of West Portal from Claremont Avenue and Taraval Street. (Courtesy San Francisco History Center, San Francisco Public Library.)

Horses pull the plow, clearing the land at Portola Drive as construction of Twin Peaks Boulevard begins on December 22, 1915. The Twin Peaks Tunnel, designed for rapid railway transit, was considered too dangerous and uneconomical to include an auto roadway. So, a road beginning 900 feet east of the San Miguel Rancho and connecting Portola Drive was begun, wrapping around Twin Peaks. (Courtesy private collection.)

Twin Peaks Boulevard, running from Portola Drive up and around the peaks in a figure eight, was finished November 1916 and cost $57,075.77. The portion from the peaks down to Clarendon Avenue cost $26,907.97. The last portion, from Clarendon Avenue down to Clayton Street, was finished in early 1917 at a cost of $7,732. As documented in a municipal report, "From no other eminence in San Francisco can such a varied and pleasing panorama of ocean, bay, mountains and metropolis be obtained." (Courtesy private collection.)

54

Opening day of Twin Peaks Boulevard in 1918 included a traffic jam of vintage cars happily motoring around the peaks and even a few mounted police as well as speeches by dignitaries. (Courtesy private collection.)

As the new Twin Peaks Boulevard descended down from the peaks, it traveled along an existing Lincoln Road (black line on map), which went past Tank Hill all the way down to Clayton Street. Burnett Avenue intersected Lincoln Road. (Courtesy Nancy Hogan collection.)

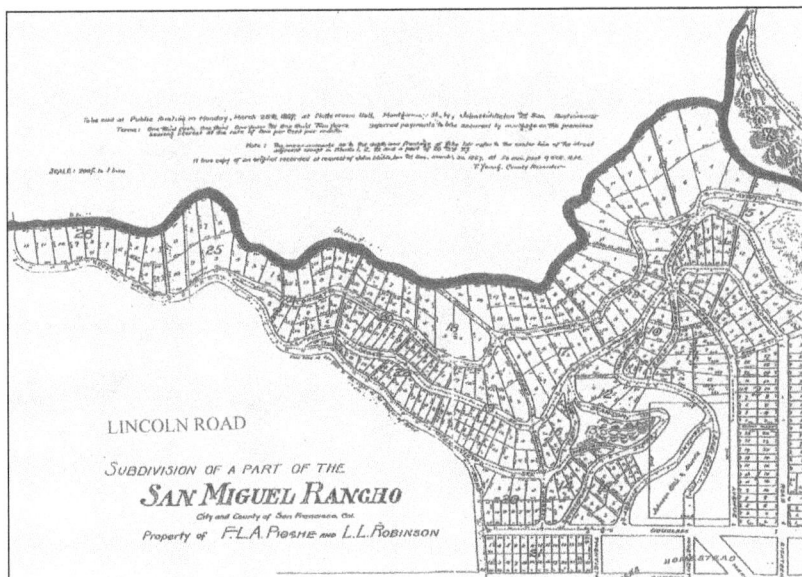

LINCOLN ROAD

SUBDIVISION OF A PART OF THE

SAN MIGUEL RANCHO
City and County of San Francisco, Cal.
Property of F. L. A. Pioshe and L. L. Robinson

A completed Twin Peaks Boulevard winds down toward Tank Hill and Clarendon Avenue in 1918. Homes are beginning to appear on the Crown, Graystone, and Villa Terraces to the right of Twin Peaks Boulevard, and a home designed by Bernard Maybeck has been built next to Tank Hill. (Courtesy private collection.)

This is the view of the last part of Twin Peaks Boulevard to be constructed, winding its way down toward Clayton Street, just past Tank Hill on the right, and straight toward the Ashbury Tank. To the left of Twin Peaks Boulevard are the Villa, Graystone, and Crown Terraces carved out on the eastern slope. (Courtesy private collection.)

Market Street ended at about Castro Street in the early 1900s. Plans were made to extend Market Street up and around Twin Peaks, and even as early as 1891, a survey was prepared for a possible route over Twin Peaks. There are many dairy farms on the slopes of Twin Peaks and into the Castro Street area in this photograph. (Courtesy private collection.)

Twin Peaks Boulevard, Corbett Avenue, and the Market Street extension can be seen in this 1940s photograph. The Miller-Joost home is on the right, tucked into the trees, just past the large houses in the foreground. The Twin Peaks School is on the slope, left of center near the white picket fence on Corbett Avenue. In 1956, Market Street was widened from Castro and Market Streets up to the connection with Portola Drive. (Courtesy private collection.)

From 1918 to 1921, private property was infringed on and homes were demolished when Market Street was extended from Falcon Street (Eighteenth Street) up to and past Corbett Avenue, becoming the Market Street extension. Real estate dealer Martin Hanson lost his battle to keep the city from cutting off some of his property. Out of anger, he erected a seven-foot-tall granite monument near Market and Corbett Streets, part of which read, "This monument is erected to peace and justice 1918–1968 A half-step in history." (Courtesy private collection.)

Martin Hanson left a letter to his friend, six-year-old Elva, inside the monument, to be opened by her in 1968. Ironically, the city decided to widen Market Street in 1956, and the monument was to be torn down. A ceremony was held, and the letter was read by Elva, now the wife of Fred Rust, 12 years earlier than intended. The letter turned out to be three copper boxes containing essays by Hanson, Thomas Paine, and Eugene Sue. (Author's collection.)

Monument of Protest to Progress of S. F. Is Razed

The Past Has Its Day

Eccentric's Last Words

By WILL STEVENS

The granite pillar of protest which eccentric Martin Hanson erected 31 years ago atop Twin Peaks, to mark his derision for progress that levels the homes of men, was jack-hammered to pieces yesterday.

Hanson, a peevish old man who despised city officials to the day of his death, would have had the last laugh yesterday had he not died 20 years earlier.

A crew of workmen under the direction of Sherman Duckel, director of public works, required an hour to find the copper box Hanson encased in the monument—a box presumably holding a mysterious message for Mrs. Elva Rust of 61 Van Ripper Lane, Orinda.

ADVICE OFFERED.

It was not Duckel, nor Henry Lutz, the granite cutter Duckel brought along, nor even Mrs. Rust herself who finally offered the advice that located the copper box and its message.

That advice came from a Twin Peaks housewife, Mrs. Juliette Reuze of 944 Corbett Ave., who good-naturedly suggested to Duckel:

"Why don't you people

HANSON'S HERITAGE — Mrs. Elva Rust yesterday finally received the mysterious message that was addressed to her 31 years ago, thanks to progress and a pair of pliers. In her hand she carries the message and a photograph of the Portola Drive area in 1920. With her are (from left) her daughter Barbara, Sherman Duckel, who has the metal container that carrie Rust, her h

MARKET STREET EXTENSION

SUBDIVISION OF A PART OF THE

SAN MIGUEL RANCHO

City and County of San Francisco, Cal.

Property of F.L.A. Pioshe AND L.L. Robinson

In the 1800s, Market Street ran from the Ferry Building toward Twin Peaks and was considered the Champs-Élysée of San Francisco, a main artery for travel and business. The board of supervisors wanted to extend Market Street as a supplement to the Twin Peaks Tunnel. The Market Street extension began at Eighteenth Street, continued to Falcon Street, on to Caselli (now Clayton) Street, then up the hill to intersect Corbett Avenue, and continued around the hill to Portola Drive. (Courtesy Nancy Hogan collection.)

This view of the Market Street extension looks south from Corwin Street. The extension was just a narrow path as it led up the hill toward Twin Peaks on September 27, 1918. There is a wooden sidewalk extending down the hill. (Courtesy private collection.)

The Market Street extension followed this path and ran parallel to and below Corbett Avenue on the eastern slope of Twin Peaks. This photograph shows the area at approximately Morgan Alley. (Courtesy private collection.)

The Market Street extension would head south, toward the house in the center of this 1918 photograph. (Courtesy private collection.)

These unidentified boys play on Falcon Street before it made way for the Market Street extension. Just above the second boy from left is the Ashbury Tank, hazy in the distance. Using that tank as a reference point, the orientation of the Market Street extension progress can be compared with the original street. (Courtesy private collection.)

These boys play on Falcon Street in 1918. The street, pointing straight toward the Ashbury Tank up on the hill, later became the Market Street extension. This is almost the same location as in the following photograph. The homes on the right in the distance are in the next image but closer. (Courtesy private collection.)

The Market Street extension project is under way at Romain Street on March 18, 1921. This is approximately the same location as the previous photograph, with the Ashbury Tank in the distance. The houses on the right can be seen on the right of the previous picture. (Courtesy private collection.)

This grocery store was once located at the corner of the Market Street extension and Romain Street. A bit of the Ashbury Tank can be seen in the upper left of this September 22, 1918, photograph. (Courtesy private collection.)

Twin Peaks School, located on Corbett Avenue, is in the top center of this 1918 photograph. Twin Peaks Boulevard runs above it, and below is a part of the Market Street extension before the road was improved. The house in the upper left with the white front porch appears on the following pages in varying stages of the extension construction. (Courtesy private collection.)

This March 18, 1921, image looks north toward Tank Hill. Horses, trucks, and backhoes work together to prepare the street. The small house with the white front porch—seen on the previous page—is visible below Tank Hill and above the horses in this image. (Courtesy private collection.)

This part of the Market Street extension, situated north of Morgan Alley, was nearing completion on June 13, 1921. This view looks back toward the construction taking place in the previous image. The same small house with the white front porch is the first house on the right of this photograph. (Courtesy private collection.)

This view of the completed Market Street extension shows the switchback right in the middle of the image. Corbett Avenue is in the upper right part of the photograph, running parallel to the Market Street extension. The house with the white front porch, located in the previous photographs, is to the right of the curve in the middle of the photograph. (Courtesy private collection.)

This 1921 view of the Market Street extension shows where it meets Corbett Avenue. This is where the tollgate was located. (Courtesy private collection.)

This is a 2012 view of the Corbett Avenue and Market Street intersection. In 1956, the Market Street extension was widened, and this portion, which was Market Street, became a parking area and access to apartments. The Market Street extension was moved farther east from this point. (Author's collection.)

Tracks were laid for streetcar use on the Market Street extension. This view looks up toward the switchback. (Courtesy private collection.)

This car travels down Clayton Street toward the switchback at the Market Street extension in 1923. The tracks have been laid, but there is no pavement yet. The Miller-Joost house can be seen where the tracks curve down to the right. (Courtesy private collection.)

A streetcar is on its way down the Market Street extension in 1923. (Courtesy private collection.)

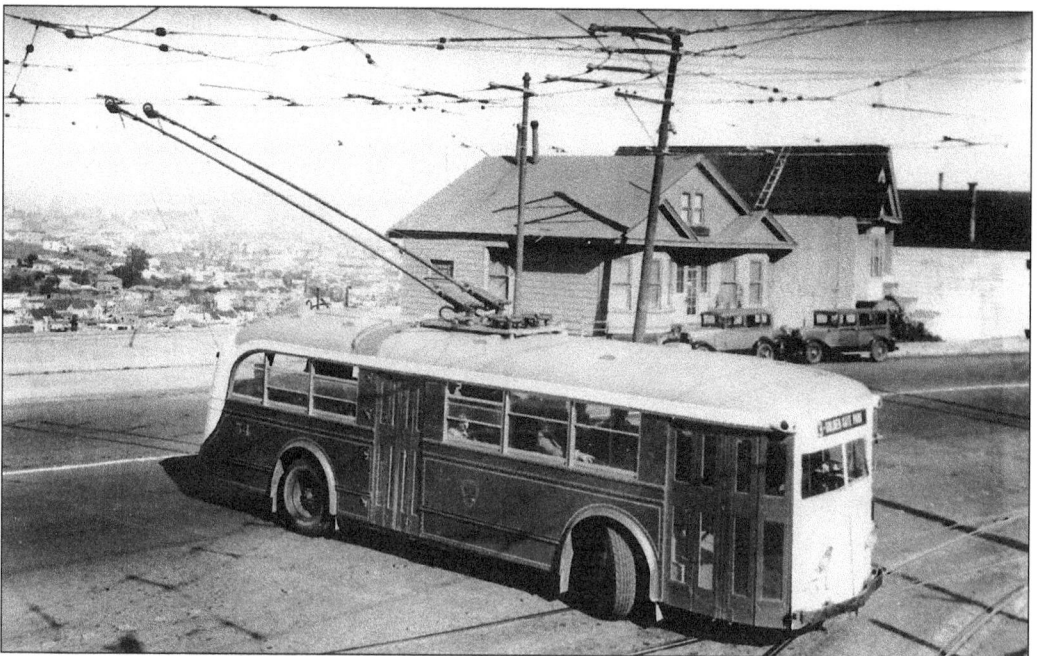

In 1935, the No. 33 trolley bus, which carried 40 passengers, turns at the switchback located at Market and Clayton Streets. (Courtesy private collection.)

Four

Settlers on the Peaks

The construction of Twin Peaks Boulevard opened the way for more settlers on the peaks. The big attractions, of course, were the views and the country ambiance of this oasis in the center of San Francisco. Noted people who have found their way to living on the slopes of the peaks are sculptress Ruth Asawa Lanier; chemist Charlie Gerchaut; district attorney Tom Lynch; writer Erskine Caldwell; Mayor Elmer Robinson; conductor Seiji Ozawa; attorney Melvin Belli; author Ruth Heller; war correspondent, chairman of UPI, and owner of the Buena Vista Winery since 1940 Frank Bartholomew; artist, actor, and puppeteer Ralph Chessé; Dean David E. Snodgrass, who created the Sixty Five Club, a distinguished faculty at Hastings College of the Law; and the Kilpatrick family, who established the Kilpatrick's bakery, to name a few.

In the 1950s, novelist and playwright Mark Harris wrote about his neighbors on Twin Peaks, "They're not a writers' colony, but one feels that almost every one writes a bit. They're not people who center their lives on their neighborhood. They don't go to local bars, and they do their shopping downtown. These people wouldn't live on the Avenues, nor in just any suburb, though they might live in a college town." Artist Ruth Asawa Lanier enjoyed the Twin Peaks area because "it has all the qualities of North Beach but none of the involvement." District attorney Tom Lynch felt that "Twin Peaks is where you find the best urban view in the world. And I can be anywhere in town—anywhere at all—in ten minutes." In the 1930s, one realtor called the area "the poor man's Telegraph Hill."

Many of the early homes in the Clarendon Heights area ranged from rustic cabins to ornate Spanish haciendas. The homes that were built in the 1930s and 1940s on the Villa, Graystone, and Crown Terraces reflected a mixture of Art Deco, mountain, and contemporary styles. The homes in Midtown, which was developed in the 1950s, had a more contemporary design. In Corbett Heights, along Corbett Avenue, apartments, duplexes, and homes replaced the dairy farms.

Dairy and produce farmers were the earliest settlers on Twin Peaks. The old Corbett Road was extended along the eastern slope of Twin Peaks in 1860, and among the first dairy farmers was Anna Miller's family. She married Behrend Joost, who was known as the "Father of Southwest San Francisco" and the "Grand Old Man of Twin Peaks" because of his work with the electric railway and his Mountain Spring Water Company on Twin Peaks. (Courtesy private collection.)

This sloped-roof mountain home was built on Clarendon Heights in 1910 before Twin Peaks Boulevard was constructed. Access to the site was by Lincoln Road, which came up from Clayton Street, past Tank Hill, and split up to the right toward Sutro Forest and to the left toward Twin Peaks. When Twin Peaks Boulevard was extended down to Clayton Street, it ran past this home on the old Lincoln Road. (Author's collection.)

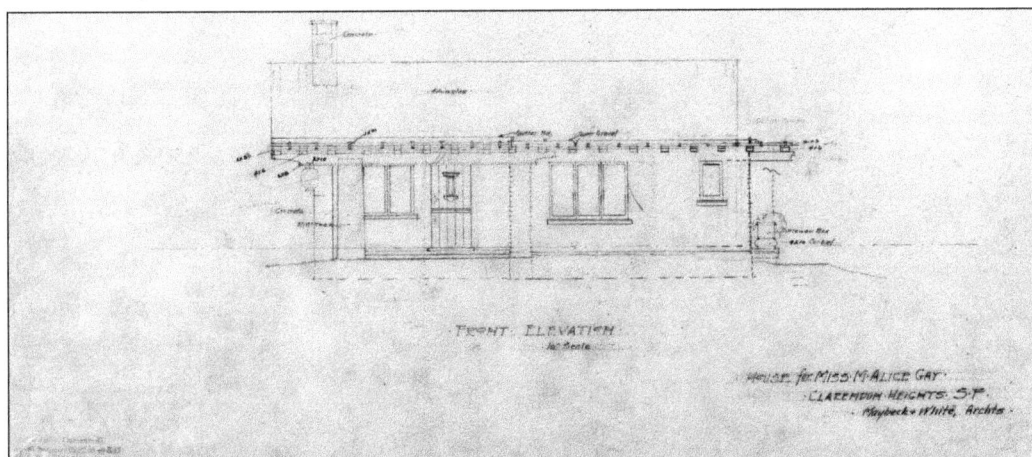

Bernard Maybeck, a renowned architect who designed the Palace of Fine Arts for the 1915 Panama Pacific International Exposition, designed the home at 196 Twin Peaks Boulevard in 1917 for Alice Gay. She insisted that it not cost more than $4,000. Maybeck satisfied her stipulation but did not include as many of his woodcarvings and spectacular motifs as he generally did. This is a design of that home by Maybeck. (Courtesy the Bernard Maybeck Records at the University of California, Berkeley, the University of California Berkeley Environmental Design Archives.)

Maybeck's Arts and Crafts style was enhanced by the Northern California redwood he used in his designs. The Alice Gay house has redwood throughout, and there is a beamed ceiling in the large living room. It is a "small rustic cottage, which incorporates living space with outdoors charm," read *Here Today, San Francisco's Architectural Heritage*, written by Roger Olmstead and T.H. Watkins in 1969. (Courtesy the Bernard Maybeck Records at the University of California, Berkeley, the University of California Berkeley Environmental Design Archives.)

Edward Raymond Moffitt built the highest house on Twin Peaks in 1920. He wrote, "The lot we found was mostly rock, so a foundation was a simple matter. We set redwood 4x4s on the rock and framed up from there." This is the lot in 1915 before the home was built. At the bottom of the hill on the right are the mountain homes built in 1910 and 1911. (Courtesy private collection.)

The lots that Moffitt bought were just up the hill from Twin Peaks Boulevard, behind the 1910 mountain home. In this photograph, Moffitt stands on the beginnings of his home, with Sutro Forest and empty land behind him. (Author's collection.)

Moffitt unloads lumber from his wagon on Twin Peaks Boulevard in 1919, next to a home that was built in 1911. There were no roads up the hill to his lots, so at first, he used a boom and pulley to hoist the lumber up the hill. Growing tired of this process, he then enlisted the help of his friends, and they carved out Mountain Spring Avenue. (Author's collection.)

Edward Moffitt and friends carve out Mountain Spring Avenue, off Twin Peaks Boulevard in 1920. The Bernard Maybeck home, built for Alice Gay in 1917, is in the center of this photograph right above the moving car, next to the Clarendon Heights Water Tank on Tank Hill. The mountain home, built in 1910, is right behind the workers on the left with all the windows. (Author's collection.)

From left to right, Regina Tissot, Paul Tissot (great-grandson of the first alcalde of San Francisco, Don Francisco de Haro), Theresa Moffitt, Paul Tissot Jr., Joyce Tissot, and Alice Moffitt sit on rocks at the site of the Moffitt home on Clarendon Heights in 1920. Sutro Forest is in the background. (Author's collection.)

Moffitt and his wife, Babe, built every part of this home themselves. Their water tank "was filled by a ¾ inch pipe that was connected to the pump of a good friend and neighbor . . . who allowed us to use his pump. When we did take a bath we fired up a wood and coal stove with four five-gallon cans of water set to heat. Light was by candle, no telephone, what a simple, beautiful life!" (Author's collection.)

In 1930, after a four-year stay in Monterey, where Moffitt built the Hacienda de Los Amigos (the Santa Catalina School for Girls) for Harold Mack, Moffitt returned to San Francisco, where he added a Spanish Colonial touch to his own hacienda on the peaks. He raised the original cottage, adding 54,000 reinforced bricks, and then constructed another building for his furniture workshop. This is a 1939 view of the Moffitt home. (Author's collection.)

The completed Moffitt home, now looking more like a Spanish castle, has incredible views of the city toward the north, east, and south. Edward Raymond Moffitt and his wife hiked all over Twin Peaks before 1920, searching for the spot with the best views. (Author's collection.)

Paula, Pat, Babe, and Edward Moffitt stand outside their home on Twin Peaks. Edward was not only the builder of the highest home on Twin Peaks in 1920, he was also a prolific furniture maker, creating hundreds of beautiful pieces of furniture for San Francisco and Monterey residents. He was recognized as the first commercial ship model builder in California. (Author's collection.)

Caretakers were hired to live in Sutro Forest to chase out vagrants that used to camp in the forest and build campfires, which was a danger to the forest. There was a tremendous fire in 1899 that burned 60 acres, and in 1934, a fire burned 10 acres and required 400 firemen to put it out. Pictured here on March 1939 are caretakers Dermalder, his wife, and Walsh on the left with an unidentified man at right. (Author's collection.)

The Howard G. Makelim house was built in 1935. Makelim owned a small, very successful repair shop in San Francisco in 1922. In 1937, Makelim made headlines by ridding the neighborhood of a hungry raccoon that was eating all the goldfish in backyard pools. He used an ingenious trap attached to a bell in his home. As was reported in the *Chronicle*, "Makelim was happy. Neighbors were enthusiastic. Goldfish breathed more easily." (Author's collection.)

This home was designed and built by Levon Nishkian in 1936. He immigrated to the United States in 1890. Nishkian was a civil engineer who designed, among other things, the Loews Warfield Theatre at Market and Taylor Streets, the two Gunst Buildings, parts of the Hetch Hetchy water system, and more than 200 Bank of America buildings in California. (Author's collection.)

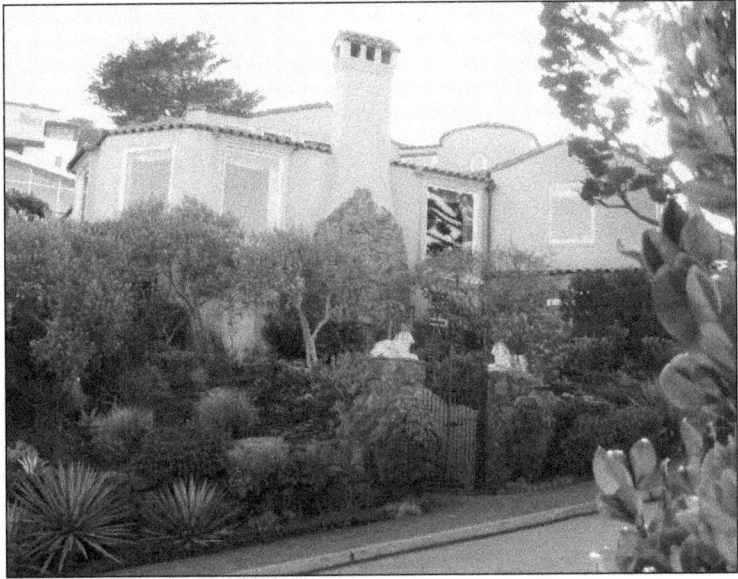

This 1931 Spanish-style home, located on Mountain Spring Avenue on Clarendon Heights, was built by architect George DeColmesnil. Architect Clarence A. Tantau redesigned it in 1935. He was known for his Spanish-style architecture. Well-known furniture builder Edward Moffitt, who lived across from this home, built a few of the interior doors. (Author's collection.)

This was the Bartholomew home on Clarendon Heights. Frank Bartholomew, a war correspondent and chairman of UPI, had also owned the Buena Vista Winery since 1940. The Buena Vista Winery is the oldest commercial winery in California, founded in 1857. Bartholomew replanted some of the original vineyards in 1941, and when he sold it in 1968, he retained most of those original vineyards to form Hacienda Wine Cellars. (Author's collection.)

Adolph Sutro's grandson Adolph Gilbert Sutro built this medieval/English country manor home (La Avenzada) at the summit of Clarendon Heights Hill in 1935. Designed by architect Harold Stoner, it was the highest home in the area in the 1930s. The mansion was sold to the American Broadcasting Company in 1948 for $125,000, and the first television show from KGO-TV premiered in May 1949. It was later demolished to make room for the current Sutro Tower. (San Francisco History Center, San Francisco Public Library.)

This *Examiner* photograph by Tom King shows the lions in front of Adolph Gilbert Sutro's La Avenzada at the summit of Clarendon Heights. The elder Adolph Sutro also had lions at the entrance gates to his Land's End property at the far west end of San Francisco, west of the Golden Gate. Designer Harold Stoner "specialized in atmospheric make believe," as reported by the *Chronicle*'s John King. (Author's collection.)

Harold Stoner designed this Spanish Revival estate located on the corner of Twin Peaks Boulevard and Clarendon Avenue in 1938. The outer walls are textured stucco, which give its appearance an adobe look. Stoner designed many homes in the west area of Twin Peaks as well as the two on Clarendon Heights. (Author's collection.)

Another example of the Spanish Revival homes built on Twin Peaks is this home on Mountain Spring Avenue, as it appeared on a 1936 Christmas card with faces of the Moody family. It was built in 1932 and has since been remodeled. (Author's collection.)

This large adobe-style home at the top of Villa Terrace was built in 1927. It is terraced down the hill toward Clayton Street. Villa is still a dirt road in this late 1920s photograph. (Courtesy private collection.)

Fernando Nelson & Sons built this Art Deco home on Villa Terrace in 1940. Fernando Nelson and his sons built more than 4,000 homes from 1876 until post World War II and were mostly known for the Victorian homes that they built in the Castro district in the 1870s, 1880s, and 1890s and the development next to the western entrance of the Twin Peaks Tunnel in West Portal. (Author's collection.)

One of the earliest homes on the terraces, this Craftsman-style home was built in 1913. During the Depression, this house was actually divided into two homes and then later returned to its original condition. The first owners were the Simons family. Instead of facing the house toward the downtown view, the owners turned it toward their Simons-Fout Brick Company, located on or near where Twin Peaks School was built. Tank Hill can be seen above the house to the left. (Courtesy Pat and Rita A. da Luz collection.)

The Midtown development in the 1950s was dedicated to building unattached homes while maintaining access to views. The streets are named with views in mind, such as Skyview, Cityview, Longview, and Knollview. Most of the homes were built on one side of each street to maximize views. The homes, averaging 1,200 square feet, were sold for $13,000 to $20,000 in those days. (Author's collection.)

Five

THE TERRACES

In 1912, Mayor Sunny Jim Rolph asked voters to approve the city's purchase of most of Twin Peaks in an attempt to preserve its natural beauty. The $200,000 bond issue failed to get the necessary two-thirds majority. However, Mayor Rolph raised funds for the city to buy the uppermost part of the peaks by selling the property in the Almshouse tract (between the Sunset District and the westerly side of Almshouse Road) for a total of $110,000. This allowed Twin Peaks Boulevard and Christmas Tree Point to be constructed on property that the city bought from Wells Fargo and Company, formerly the Collamore Tract, and property of Mary Craig (some of the land was donated by Wells Fargo and Mary Craig). The cost of these 29 acres was $78,550. The city already owned the property surrounding the Twin Peaks Reservoir. The slope below Twin Peaks Boulevard remained in private hands. Today, the summit is part of the 31 acres of land called the Twin Peaks Natural Area, managed and owned by the San Francisco Recreational and Parks Department.

In the 1930s, the eastern terraces were carved on the steep hilly eastern slope of Twin Peaks leading up to Twin Peaks Boulevard. Each terrace provides magnificent city views. Construction on the Midtown Terraces on the west and south sides of Twin Peaks began in 1953. These terraces provide views of the Pacific Ocean, Forest Knolls, Sutro Forest, and San Bruno Mountain.

Harold Gilliam wrote in the *Chronicle* in 1962 that the construction of apartments and private homes on the eastern slope of Twin Peaks had destroyed the image of Twin Peaks, which had been a symbol of the city for more than a century. Twin Peaks appeared in most historical paintings and photographs of San Francisco. It could be seen in the background of the Spanish village of Yerba Buena and the Gold Rush settlement of the 1850s and 1860s. Twin Peaks remained unchanged until 1906. Gilliam observed that Market Street was distinguished from other city main streets by having the Ferry Building at one end and Twin Peaks at the other.

This late 1800s photograph of the northeastern slope of Twin Peaks shows Tank Hill with Lincoln Road running past it. The curving old Corbett Road is just to the left of center in this image, beneath the forest. Villa, Graystone, and Crown Terraces were later located in the upper left of the photograph, where the forest is above Corbett Road. (Courtesy private collection.)

This 1923 view of the terraces shows them nestled beneath Tank Hill, just off Twin Peaks Boulevard. Villa Terrace winds down from the right corner, Graystone Terrace is next in the middle, and Crown Terrace is at upper left. The Pemberton Steps cut through the terraces from Clayton Street (not seen) up through Villa Terrace, Graystone Terrace, and Crown Terrace. (Courtesy San Francisco History Center, San Francisco Public Library.)

This view of Pemberton Place was taken from Fout Avenue. Fout Avenue was later named Graystone Terrace. This whole section of the Pioche and Robinson Subdivision was called Ashbury Park. The three people pictured here are out to enjoy the day in 1908. This parcel of land was sold to the City of San Francisco on January 23, 1915. The owners of the Simons-Fout Brick Company, plus Charles E. Pemberton, Elizabeth Pemberton, and William Samuel Pemberton, signed the contract. The land just to the right was later built on (see next photograph) in 1911, reportedly by the Pemberton family. On the original map of the Pioche and Robinson Subdivision, it looks like Pemberton Place was originally called Opal Alley. (Courtesy Pat Taber and Rita A. da Luz collection.)

Pemberton Place steps extend up the hill from Clayton Street, up through the carved-out terraces, in this early-20th-century photograph. The Simons-Fout Brick Company owned Pemberton and the acreage around it, called Ashbury Park Tract, which was part of the Pioche and Robinson Subdivision. The home in the upper right supposedly belonged to the Cyril Pemberton family and was built in 1911. The lower section of the home abuts where Villa Terrace is now. (Courtesy private collection.)

This 1917 photograph, taken from Clayton Street, looks up to the Simons home in the center of the image, just to the left of Tank Hill. The Pemberton Place steps begin where the structure is on the left side of Clayton Street. Twin Peaks Boulevard would be finished this year, running behind the Simons home on what used to be Lincoln Road. There are tracks on the road for the electric streetcar. The switchback at Falcon and Clayton Streets was behind the photographer. (Courtesy Pat Taber and Rita A. da Luz collection.)

The Twin Peaks Grammar School sits in the center on Corbett Avenue. Graystone Terrace leads up to the school on the right, while the Market Street extension winds up the hill on the left. This late 1920s photograph shows where the terraces would eventually be developed in the acreage to the right of the school. (Courtesy private collection.)

This is the entrance to Villa Terrace from Twin Peaks Boulevard in 1941. It is still unpaved. (Courtesy private collection.)

This 1942 photograph, down the upper part of Villa Terrace from Twin Peaks Boulevard, offers a view of the open hillside with a few more homes on it. Villa is the first of the terraces up from Clayton Street. Because these streets are on the slope of Twin Peaks, they have been terraced, as have some of the buildings. (Courtesy private collection.)

The adobe building at the top of Villa Terrace, pictured on the right, is terraced down the hill to Clayton Street. It was built in 1927. This 1942 view looks back up Villa Terrace toward Twin Peaks Boulevard. (Courtesy private collection.)

Villa Terrace is a fairly
straight street in this
1942 photograph, until
it reaches Pemberton
Place, just beyond
the bushes on the
left. Then it becomes
a curvy country
road. Tank Hill sits
majestically above the
terraces. The white
building on the left
is terraced down the
hill from Graystone
Terrace to Villa
Terrace. (Courtesy
private collection.)

In 1949, real estate developer Grace Perego planned to construct six multistory apartment houses with 54 units on Graystone Terrace. The neighbors protested, and the planning commission compromised by leaving the Perego property in the second-residential classification and classifying the block between the Graystone and Villa Terraces as first-residential, with apartment buildings banned. Grace Perego apartments are on Graystone Terrace at the intersection with Villa Terrace. (Author's collection.)

In 1952, Grace Perego attempted to turn the small Crown Terrace into a thoroughfare for access from her apartment complex to Twin Peaks Boulevard instead of using Burnett Avenue, which was undergoing repairs due to water seepage. The residents of Crown Terrace fought back by blocking Grace Perego's car, the white car in the foreground. Herbert Eugene "Herb" Caen wrote many articles about the battle in his daily column, which appeared in his 1949 book *Baghdad-by-the-Bay*. (Courtesy *San Francisco Examiner*.)

The Crown Terrace residents and their attorney Jake Ehrlich won their battle against Perego. Judge William Thomas Sweigert acknowledged that Crown Terrace is a lane that has never been used as a thoroughfare, and the Perego residents have not been inconvenienced. He also stated that, if at any time, the Grace Perego residents are inconvenienced by repair of Burnett Avenue, the court will restrain any obstruction of Crown Terrace. Domestic peace and tranquility returned to the neighborhood. (Courtesy San Francisco History Center, San Francisco Public Library.)

Seen in this late 1930s photograph looking northwest from Twin Peaks toward Clarendon Heights and Sutro Forest is the acreage that eventually became Midtown Terrace. Twin Peaks Reservoir can be seen on the right side of the image with the Golden Gate and Golden Gate Bridge off in the distance behind it. (Courtesy private collection.)

This is a 2012 view of the same location as the previous photograph. Summit Reservoir is seen on the upper left, and a little of Twin Peaks Reservoir is visible through the trees on the right. (Author's collection.)

The Standard Building Company, owned by Carl and Fred Gellert, and the Panorama Development Company began construction of 817 single-family two- and three-bedroom homes on the west of Twin Peaks in 1954. The western slope was mapped into seven different levels, all with views of Sutro Forest, Laguna Honda Reservoir, Mount Davidson, St. Francis Wood, Forest Hill, and the Pacific Ocean. (Courtesy San Francisco History Center, San Francisco Public Library.)

Construction on the 150 acres of land making up Midtown Terrace began on Midcrest Drive on April 13, 1953. Summit Reservoir was built in 1954 on Clarendon Heights, and Twin Peaks Reservoir can be seen in the upper left corner. Twin Peaks is above the homes on Midcrest Drive, and Portola Drive runs east to west below Midcrest Drive. (Courtesy San Francisco History Center, San Francisco Public Library.)

96

Six

LIFE ON TWIN PEAKS

Twin Peaks means many things to the people of San Francisco. It has spectacular views and hiking opportunities, attracting locals and visitors. The neighborhoods on its slopes have a distinctive country feel to them. It has three main reservoirs, Sutro Tower, and the towers located at Christmas Tree Point. The Christmas Tree Point towers are San Francisco's Central Radio Station, providing communications support for municipal police and fire departments, the 911 dispatch system, the sheriff's office, Office of Emergency Management, the Public Utilities Commission, the district attorney's office, and the Unified School District.

Centrally located, Twin Peaks can be seen by most of San Francisco, particularly by the downtown, or eastern side, of the city. As a result, many events and causes have been celebrated on Twin Peaks to be enjoyed by the whole city. The celebration of the building of the Twin Peaks Reservoir in 1912 was the first of these events, complete with picnics, dances, diving exhibitions, and speeches. The grand opening of Twin Peaks Boulevard in 1918 up on the peaks featured speeches and parades of cars. Annually, the San Francisco Pride Celebration displays a large pink triangle on the eastern side of Twin Peaks below Christmas Tree Point, and the AIDS awareness festivities include a large red ribbon on the eastern slope. The height and twisty character of Twin Peaks Boulevard makes it a great location for races that have been held on and around the peaks, such as the April Fool's Run, the Bay Bikers' Seven Hells of San Francisco ride, the Mash Twin Peaks Time Trial, and even wheeled luge races.

Several movies have been filmed on Twin Peaks. *Experiment in Terror* (1962), starring Lee Remick and Glen Ford, was filmed on Clarendon Heights. One of the characters lived at 100 St. Germain Avenue, and that house appeared in the movie. *Vertigo* (1958) featured city views from Christmas Tree Point. *Copycat*, starring Sigourney Weaver and Holly Hunter, was also filmed on Twin Peaks. Many car commercials have featured steep Glenbrook Avenue sloping down to Mountain Spring Avenue with the city view as its backdrop.

This is the spectacular lookout point, located just north of Eureka Peak. It is known as Christmas Tree Point because, in 1951, in response to the fire department's annual Christmas decoration contest in which fire houses were decorated all over the city, the San Francisco Police Department erected a tall Christmas tree for everyone in the city to enjoy, as seen in this photograph. The fire department tradition only lasted for three years, from 1948 to 1950, but the first year, the grand prize-winning firehouse received $1,000, and they were only allowed to spend $50 on decorations. This Christmas tree became the city's official Christmas tree. There was caroling and refreshments at the base of the tree as the beautiful views surrounded it all. (Courtesy private collection.)

Crowds gather on Twin Peaks at Christmas Tree Point and elsewhere on the slopes to watch the Graf Zeppelin, an airship, pass by in 1930. Because the Graf Zeppelin circled the globe, there was much excitement wherever it would appear in the 1920s and 1930s. (Author's collection.)

When the Graf Zeppelin reached San Francisco via Newfoundland and New York in 1930, it had completed a round-the-world flight of 33,500 miles in two years and 34 days. Spectators lined the peaks to watch for the zeppelin, which is seen in the upper left corner of this photograph. (Author's collection.)

In 1941, two Rhesus monkeys, a male and a female, escaped from the Hooper Foundation Laboratories and ended up on Twin Peaks on top of a roof. The Hooper Foundation was located on Parnassus Avenue, just below Clarendon Heights, and was part of the UCSF campus. (Author's collection.)

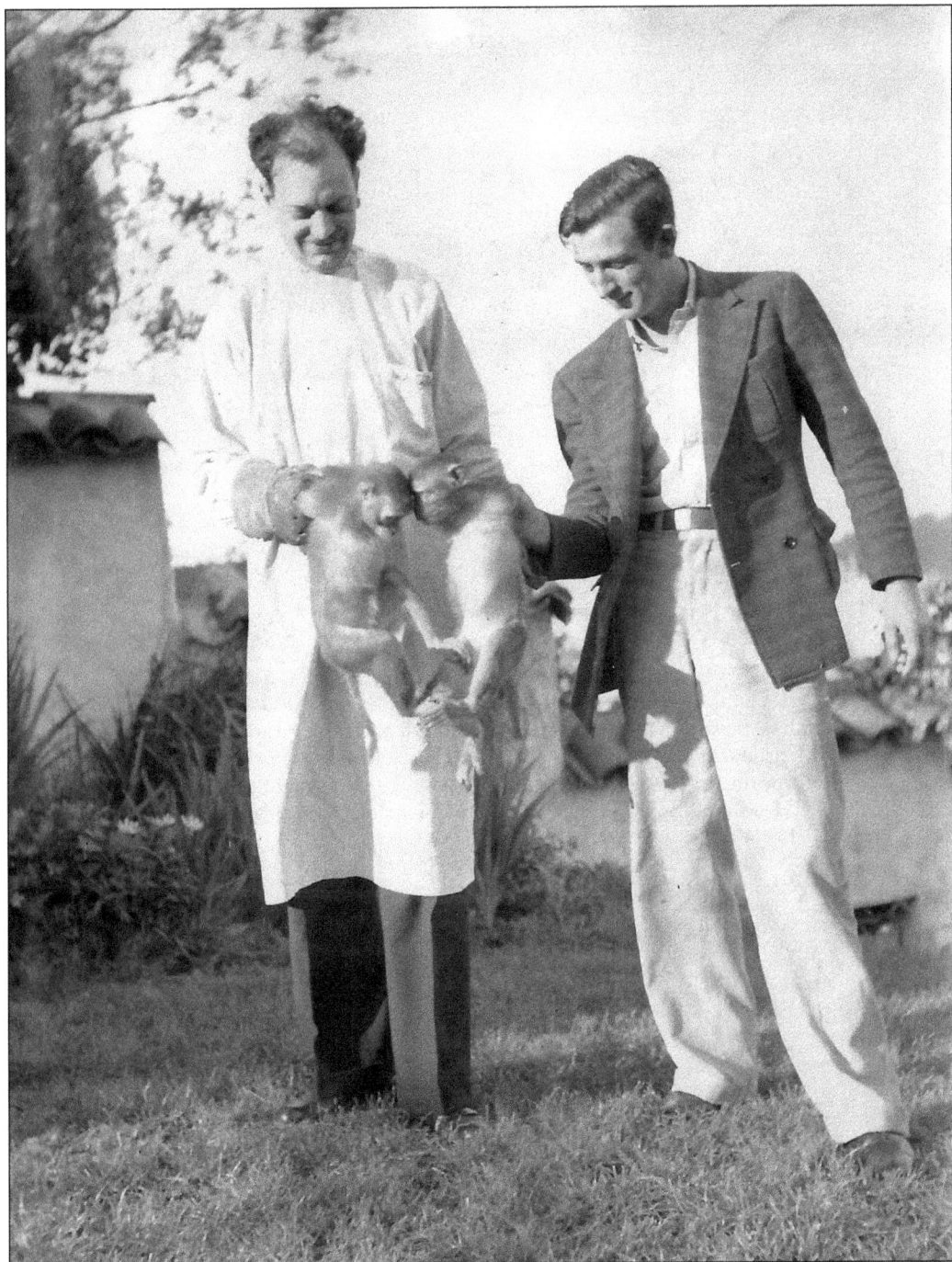

These two men from the Hooper Foundation finally captured the monkeys. The doctor on the left is Dr. Paul Valdez. The Hooper Foundation, the first medical research foundation in the United States to become part of a university (in 1914), was established in memory of George Williams Hooper, a San Francisco lumber merchant and philanthropist. (Author's collection.)

Twin Peaks resident Edward Moffitt designed, patented, and built a rat racetrack equipped with six treadmills, dials, buzzers, trick lights, and bells. He scientifically nurtured his rats in an effort to create a faster-running rat. What may sound like a wacky idea caught the fancy of many people, including several leading US and European city newspapers. (Author's collection.)

Moffitt's invention was even filmed by Paramount Studios for a movie short about "unusual hobbies." Schoolchildren viewing the rat race in this 1947 Associated Press image are fascinated by the rats and the mechanism. The man on the left is a Paramount Studios photographer. (Author's collection.)

Edward Moffitt and his family and friends started their own tradition of singing and marching up to Twin Peaks on Easter Sunday, complete with guitar, harmonica, and violin to avoid the crowds on Mount Davidson. Dick Chase reported in the *Chronicle* in 1942, "All that was lacking was a trumpeter today as the residents of the east slope of Twin Peaks prepared to hold their second annual Easter Sunrise Services on the North Peak, above their homes." (Author's collection.)

The Convent of the Good Shepherd Guild sponsored a Twin Peaks house tour of nine homes in the 1950s. The funds raised were used to help girls in trouble. Mrs. Norman Reed, on the left, with Bill Reed and Mrs. Frank Fontes visit the Edward Moffitt home on Mountain Spring Avenue. (Author's collection.)

Afton Lewis Giacomini, a member of the Ninety-Nines, an international organization of women pilots, was flying with her instructor in 1930. She had a forced landing on Twin Peaks. Neither pilot was injured and her plane, a Kinner, was taken back to Mills Field for repairs. The plane was fixed up and painted, but unfortunately, as the finishing touches were added, a spark from a short in an electric wire ignited the plane. (Courtesy San Francisco History Center, San Francisco Public Library.)

The 1924 Olympic cyclist James S. Armando stands with Pat Moffitt at the Moffitt home on Clarendon Heights. Armando also was the Connecticut champion in 1932 and pedaled up Mountain Spring Avenue on Clarendon Heights in June 1938. On June 27, 1936, he was the first man to bicycle up Mount Washington in New Hampshire, the highest peak in the northeastern United States at 6,288 feet. (Author's collection.)

Pictured here is a 1951 snowfall-painted Twin Peaks. While it was rare, enough snow fell on Twin Peaks and San Francisco in 1882, 1887, 1962, and 1976 to make snowballs. A snowstorm on January 12, 1868, inspired the *Alta California* to report, "Snow covered all the roofs and sidewalks even in the lower part of town, and the hills were for the first time in years completely whitened. The effect produced upon the city was to us in California startlingly beautiful." (Courtesy private collection.)

Snowfall on Twin Peaks on February 28, 1951, attracts San Franciscans, who rarely get a chance to play in the snow. (Author's collection.)

Neighborhood kids slide down the steep sidewalk on Glenbrook Avenue in Clarendon Heights in 1951. This sidewalk is made of brick, and the snow clung to it, making for a fun, unusual experience for Twin Peaks children. (Author's collection.)

Workers take a lunch break while enjoying the views at Christmas Tree Point in the late 1930s. The Bay Bridge, which opened in 1936, can be seen behind them. (Courtesy private collection.)

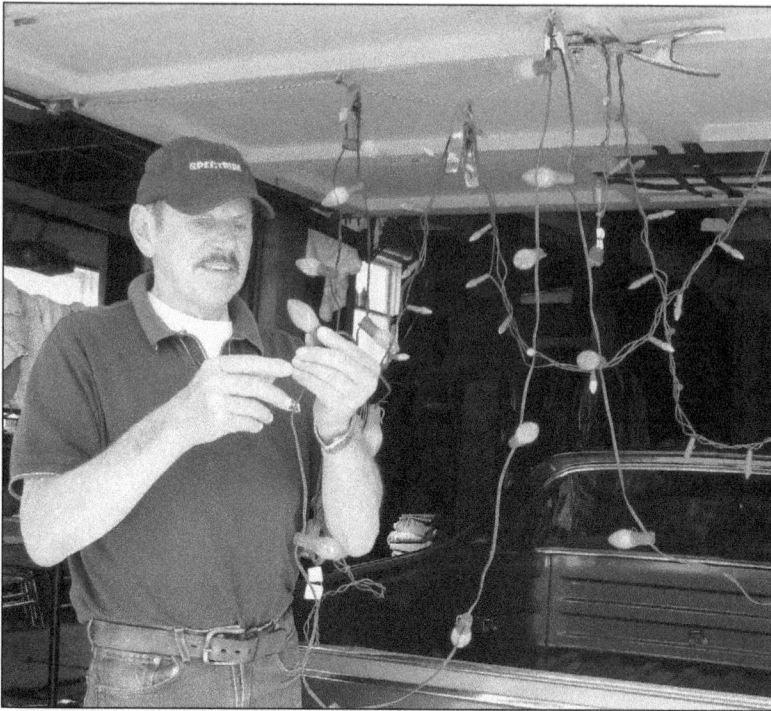

Villa Terrace resident Soc Oulson prepares Christmas lights to decorate Villa Terrace homes. Villa Terrace has hosted a spectacular holiday light display for the past 30 years with beautiful decorations on homes on the street, mostly created by Oulson. (Author's collection.)

The Villa Sinfonia violinists have played carols every year on Villa Terrace for the past 30 years. Throngs of neighbors and their friends turn out to join in the singing and enjoy the music and beautiful light displays. The residents of Villa Terrace generously donated money in 1994 to help start the Villa Sinfonia Foundation, a nonprofit music organization. (Author's collection.)

In 1985, a committee headed by Crown Terrace resident Edith Fried and Mayor Diane Feinstein renovated Christmas Tree Point with walls of indigenous stone to serve as an official greeting place for visitors to San Francisco. Here, Mayor Feinstein presents an award to Edith Fried for her efforts on refurbishing Christmas Tree Point. Michael Painter was the architect who designed the wall. (Courtesy Edith Fried collection.)

After the dedication of the new wall, balloons were released in celebration. Edith Fried also created a beautiful public garden at the corner of Twin Peaks Boulevard and Clarendon Avenue for which she won a beautification award in 2000 from San Francisco Beautiful, whose mission is "to create, enhance, and maintain the unique beauty and livability of San Francisco." Likewise, the Bernstein family planted trees just below Summit Reservoir, for which they received a commendation from the city. (Courtesy Edith Fried collection.)

The Pemberton Place steps start at Clayton Street and rise upward through the terraces to Crown Terrace. Heavy rains damaged the steps in 1982 and 1983, and the Department of Public Works installed beams to prevent further decay. In 2000, neighbors (spearheaded by Pemberton resident Myra Ruskin) worked with the city to redesign a section of the steps from Graystone Terrace down to Villa Terrace and farther down to Clayton Street. (Courtesy Nancy Hogan collection.)

Nancy Hogan and members of the Twin Peaks Improvement Association worked for 10 years to complete the Pemberton Place steps project. The original steps were two parallel flights of steps with a garden in between. The new portion is one wider set. It is terra-cotta in color with a brick pattern stamped into the composite. In 2002, Rodney Ruskin presented a drinking fountain that was added to the steps just below Villa Terrace in memory of his late wife, Myra. (Author's collection.)

The Sutro Tower was built next to the original ABC TV tower, which was later torn down in 1972. Both the ABC tower and the Sutro Tower were erected in the location of the mansion built by Adolph Gilbert Sutro in the 1930s. The Sutro mansion was torn down to accommodate this new tower. The completed Sutro Tower is 977 feet high and provides radio, television, and high-definition television broadcasts as well as other communication services. (Author's collection.)

This tower, located on a hill that sits between Twin Peaks and Mount Sutro, is operated by Sutro Tower, Inc. (STI), and owned by the KTVU, KRON, KPIX, and KGO TV stations. All other stations are tenants of STI. There was a lot of controversy surrounding this improvement; seismic stability, humming wires, electronic interference, sandblasting, possible electromagnetic radiation in the area, and maintenance of structural integrity were some of the concerns raised by residents. (Author's collection.)

In 1934, these children play amidst the rocks and boulders at the Moffitt home on Twin Peaks. From left to right, they are (first row) Paula Moffitt and two unidentified friends; (second row) Pat Moffitt, Mitzi Perkins, and an unidentified friend. (Author's collection.)

Children and pet dog Gino play on Mountain Spring Avenue in front of the Moffitt home at 34 Mountain Spring Avenue in 1956. (Author's collection.)

112

These children stand amidst rocks on Twin Peaks, dressed up to celebrate the opening of the Golden Gate Bridge in 1937. San Franciscans dressed up in Spanish and pioneer garb and walked across the bridge on its opening day. Pictured from left to right are Pat Moffitt, Mitzi Perkins, Paula Moffitt, Fritzi Glauser, and Louie Rappetto. (Author's collection.)

These Villa Terrace children play on a neighbor's doghouse in 1951. On the roof are, from left to right, Larry Lucchetti, Kenta Duffy, Greg Duffy, Brad Duffy, Sandy Christo, and Dahrl Hogan. Standing in front is Bob Hackney. The resident dog would stroll down to the University of California, San Francisco by himself and ride in the elevators until his owner, Dr. Newton, retrieved him. (Courtesy Nancy Hogan collection.)

In this April 14, 1919, image, construction is almost finished on the Twin Peaks Grammar School. John Reid Jr., the designer of the school, was associated with the Willis Polk and Daniel Burnham firm. He attended University of California, Berkeley and the Ecole de Beaux Arts and ended up as the city architect. He also built the Landmark Building at 170 Fell Street and 135 Van Ness Avenue, now the Newton Tharp School and High School of Commerce. (Courtesy San Francisco History Center, San Francisco Public Library.)

Students at the Twin Peaks Grammar School perform in the operetta *Spring Glow* in recognition of Public Education Week in 1929. These children are, from left to right (kneeling) Joan Elliott; (standing) Patricia Moffitt and Jimmie Elliott. (Author's collection.)

The 1946 Twin Peaks Grammar School kindergarten class poses on the incline of Iron Alley, which runs alongside the school. Dahrl Hogan is the last child on the right in the second row. (Courtesy Nancy Hogan collection.)

Children from the Twin Peaks Grammar School have hiked up the hill and now pose for the camera on Mountain Spring Avenue in the 1950s. Marion Bernstein remembers how her children used to walk down the hill on their way to Twin Peaks Grammar School in the 1950s, past moth-eaten goats and mules. Then they would have to hike back up to their house at the top of Clarendon Heights. (Author's collection.)

This is a photograph of a first-grade class at Twin Peaks School in 1951. Nancy Hogan, who later was a member of the Twin Peaks Improvement Association and was instrumental in the improvements on Pemberton Steps, is in the second row, far left. The group poses outside of the school at the foot of Iron Alley. (Courtesy Nancy Hogan collection.)

This is the dairy farm surrounded by trees on the eastern slope of Twin Peaks, which is clearly visible in images dated back to the 1880s. It was sold in 1949 to become the Rooftop Elementary School, the second school located on Corbett Avenue. Members of the school board take a tour of the farm in 1949. (Courtesy private collection.)

The new Rooftop Elementary School, shown here just before it opened in 1953, sits surrounded by the trees that once protected a dairy farm on Twin Peaks. The two Twin Peaks schools were combined into one. This is the Burnett Campus for grades kindergarten through fourth. The old Twin Peaks School became the Mayeda Campus for grades five through eight. It was named for beloved principal Nancy Mayeda. (Courtesy San Francisco History Center, San Francisco Public Library.)

This view toward Forest Knolls from Midtown Terrace shows the Sutro Reservoir and the acreage of land where Clarendon Alternative Elementary School (the third school in the Twin Peaks area) and the Forest Knolls development would be built. Forest Knolls sits on top of Mount Sutro. This photograph was taken by Earl Martin, an original Midtown resident. (Courtesy Forest Knolls neighborhood blog.)

In 1961, Clarendon Alternative Elementary School opened across the street from Sutro Reservoir on Clarendon Avenue. It is now the home of the Japanese Bilingual Bicultural Program. The old Almshouse Road passed by here on the way toward the Almshouse (Laguna Honda Hospital). This is also the area where Daniel Burnham envisioned a lake and villas. (Photograph by Earl Martin; courtesy Forest Knolls neighborhood blog.)

Clarendon School, which opened in 1961, educated students from the new Midtown, Forest Knolls, and Clarendon Heights neighborhoods. Even though the school had been completed, prospective students had to wait until the crossing bridge had been built over busy Clarendon Avenue before they could start attending the school. Nickie Obuhoff is on the far left in the first seated row. (Courtesy Obuhoff collection.)

Seven

MAKE BIG PLANS

"Make no little plans; they have no magic to stir men's blood and probably themselves will not be realized. Make big plans; aim high in hope and work." These were architect Daniel Burnham's thoughts in his 1910 speech before a Town Planning Conference in London as paraphrased by his San Francisco colleague architect Willis Polk. Burnham was the author of a grand "Report on a Plan for San Francisco" in 1905.

Twin Peaks has been the inspiration for many grand plans. Mayor Angelo Rossi (1931–1939) wanted to ornament the "bald cones" at the summit with trees, using WPA workers to plant the trees for $2.50 per day. The Twin Peaks Improvement Association decided against it after Edward Moffitt reminded them that the peaks were originally called Los Pechos de la Chola or "Breasts of the Indian Woman": "Now that's a name for a bare mountain, not one with trees sprouting all over it."

An 18-hole semipublic championship golf course was proposed by the S.C. Hardin Golf Construction Company in the 1920s. It was going to be situated on a large part of Sutro Forest and on the west slope of Twin Peaks, extending to Twin Peaks Boulevard in the east, toward the Affiliated Colleges in the north (they were on Parnassus Heights, where UCSF is located today), the Relief Home in the south (Laguna Honda Hospital), and Seventh Avenue in the west. Since the tunnel ran under this proposed golf course, the plan included elevators to connect with the municipal line. There was also to be a $50,000 clubhouse. Nearby residents would have "prior privileges" on this golf course. Evidently the plan was not accepted by the city. But a golf driving range did exist in the 1950s where Clarendon Elementary School is today, on Clarendon Avenue.

Located geographically in the center of San Francisco and therefore most prominent in views from all over the city, Twin Peaks has inspired many imaginative plans by well-known architects and artists. Water cascades, an observatory, a statue of St. Francis, a temple to honor pioneers and welcome those arriving from the west, and a colonnade to honor the mission-founding padres were all ideas that have been proposed. The Twin Peaks Tunnel, Twin Peaks Boulevard, and the Market Street extension were at one time fantastic dreams that were actually fulfilled.

Daniel Burnham lived in a small shack on Twin Peaks, built by Willis Polk, where he devised his elaborate plans for a report that he presented to the Association for the Improvement and Adornment of San Francisco. Mayor Eugene Edward Schmitz said, "On behalf of the citizens of San Francisco, it gives me great pleasure to accept these plans . . . they shall forever be our guiding star, as far as the beauty of the city is concerned." This 1905 photograph is most likely of Burnham's house, which was situated near to where Christmas Tree Point is located today. (Courtesy private collection.)

This is a lithographed relief map showing the system of highways, public places, and parks that architect Daniel Burnham developed and filed one day before the great 1906 earthquake. This idea would unite the city by design. His 1905 plan included a park that extended from Twin Peaks to Lake Merced. It would have been a nonstop park, as can be seen extending from the center of this map to the lower left corner. (Courtesy David Rumsey Map Collection.)

Daniel Burnham imagined the western slopes of Twin Peaks dotted with villas on the shores of a lake situated where Midtown is today. He also envisioned the Maternity, a birthing center where expectant mothers would go to benefit from the healthy environment and sea air. It was to be located in Midtown at Panorama Drive and Cityview Way above where the San Francisco Youth Guidance Center is today. Edward H. Bennett took this photograph in 1905. (Courtesy private collection.)

TWIN PEAKS, FROM CLARENDON HEIGHTS, LOOKING SOUTH

Burnham's planned Athenaeum, an academy of the arts with an open-air theater, looked west toward Lake Merced from today's Marview Drive on Twin Peaks. In his plan, a waterfall would flow through the canyon between Blue Mountain (later renamed Mount Sutro) and Clarendon Heights Hill, along Clarendon Avenue, and pool into a lake at Sutro Reservoir. The 300-foot-tall female statue, called *San Francisco*, greets visitors from Asia. This 1905 drawing appears in the "Report on a Plan for San Francisco" by Daniel Burnham and Edward H. Bennett. (Courtesy David Rumsey Map Collection.)

On the northern slope of Twin Peaks, Burnham visualized an amphitheater located above Cole Valley and bordered by Clarendon Avenue, Parnassus Avenue, Clayton Street, and Stanyan Street, overlooking the Golden Gate. The slope at left is the north side of Mount Sutro. San Francisco Bay is visible in the distance, while the Marin Headlands forming the north side of the Golden Gate is in the upper right. Horseshoes, polo matches, football, lacrosse, and other games would be played in this arena. (Courtesy David Rumsey Map Collection.)

This is the area, as seen in 1937, where Burnham planned to build his amphitheater. It was bordered by Stanyan Street on the left (running along the park), Clarendon Avenue running to the south of Tank Hill (seen at lower right), Clayton Street (not visible) to the right of Tank Hill, and Parnassus Avenue (running just below Tank Hill). (Courtesy private collection.)

These 1905 Burnham drawings show a proposed Market Street termination at the foot of Twin Peaks. The sketch below shows a wider perspective. Both sketches were included in Burnham's "Report on a Plan for San Francisco," which he presented to the Association for the Improvement and Adornment of San Francisco. The images were engraved by Sunset Press of San Francisco. (Both, courtesy David Rumsey Map Collection.)

This is a 1934 Formal Daylight Design in pastel of a proposed Twin Peaks cascade from Twin Peaks by Bernard Maybeck. Besides being an architect in the Arts and Crafts movement, he was also a professor at the University of California at Berkeley with an interest in landscapes. (Courtesy Bernard Maybeck Collection, Environmental Design Archives, University of California, Berkeley.)

This is the Bernard Maybeck proposed cascade from Twin Peaks in a nighttime setting. Maybeck was very interested in waterfalls and structures on Twin Peaks and envisioned a second Bay Bridge running alongside the current Bay Bridge. (Author's collection.)

Benny's Dream Comes True

HEROIC PROJECT—An artist's sketch of a monument to St. Francis which sculptor Beniamino Bufano, in 1936, envisioned atop Christmas Tree Point. The monument was to have towered five feet higher than the Statue of Liberty and to have been as tall as an average 16-story building. Statue was approved by Board of Supervisors and the Art Commission but work was never started.

Syndicated newspaper columnist Westbrook Pegler wrote of Bufano's stainless steel statue, in his column "Fair Enough" on August 18, 1938, that it "looks like a holdup" and also that "Mr. Bufano has been a good sport in this and I salute him, but still I insist that his St. Francis is a terrible injustice to a well loved city and saint." Bufano defended himself by saying, "I have tried to make this statue the symbol of a new religion. It symbolizes the brotherhood of man—stripped of pretense—as close to a universal interpretation as I could make it." (Author's collection.)

This 1939 San Francisco News-Call Bulletin photograph shows Bufano working on a 12-foot-high stainless steel model of the proposed 191-foot statue for Christmas Tree Point on Twin Peaks as Ann Medalie assists. He wanted to build a monument on the West Coast similar to the Statue of Liberty to represent peace and harmony. The Works Progress Administration provided him with assistants, workshops, and a salary, but the board of supervisors voted it down because of controversy about the project. (Courtesy Bancroft Library, Berkeley, California.)

A hiker makes his way up to Noe Peak (the southern peak) of Twin Peaks following the wooden step trail. This has been designated a Significant Natural Resource Area by the San Francisco Recreation and Park Department in an attempt to "preserve, restore, and enhance remnant natural areas." Despite the grand plans and the magnificent roads that have aided transportation for the city of San Francisco, plus the water and communication services centered on Twin Peaks, the peaks remain an oasis of rural beauty within an urban setting. (Author's collection.)

Visit us at
arcadiapublishing.com

www.ingramcontent.com/pod-product-compliance
Lightning Source LLC
Chambersburg PA
CBHW050550110426
42813CB00008B/2311